The Economics of
World Grain Trade

Thomas Grennes
Paul R. Johnson
Marie Thursby

The Praeger Special Studies program, through a selective worldwide distribution network, makes available to the academic, government, and business communities significant and timely research in U.S. and international economic, social, and political issues.

The Economics of
World Grain Trade

Praeger Publishers   New York   London

Library of Congress Cataloging in Publication Data

Grennes, Thomas.
    The economics of world grain trade.

    (Praeger special studies in international business,
finance, and trade)
    Includes bibliographical references and index.
    1. Grain trade.   2. Grain trade—Mathematical
models.   I. Johnson, Paul Reynold, 1929-   joint
author.   II. Thursby, Marie, joint author.   III. Title.
HD9030.5.G83   1978   382'.41'3   77-13715
ISBN 0-03-022836-0

PRAEGER SPECIAL STUDIES
200 Park Avenue, New York, N.Y., 10017, U.S.A.

Published in the United States of America in 1978
by Praeger Publishers,
A Division of Holt, Rinehart and Winston, CBS, Inc.

89   038   987654321

Concerns with the adequacy of grain supplies to feed the world seem to vary sharply with whatever short run events are taking place. Malthus observed a fairly rapid increase in population in Western Europe, and raised his famous inquiry into the nature of the food and population balance. Periodically since then, wars and other events have raised the spectre of mankind's inability to feed himself. A set of events that started in 1972 led to yet another reconsideration of this problem. The popular reaction to these events led to the preparation of this book, and our own reconsideration of the more general question of the determination of grain flows and prices in a multi-country setting.

The events leading up to 1972 and the consequences for the next several years after that are chronicled in some detail in the book. Briefly, the Soviet Union suffered a large shortfall in grain production, and large inventories of grains in North America had been disposed of. Because basic foodstuffs have a low price elasticity of demand, relatively small changes in supply will be accompanied by relatively large fluctuations in price. The shortfall of 1972 was thus coupled with a sharp price increase for grains. In some circles this price increase was interpreted as evidence that the Malthusian trap would shortly be sprung.

Grain prices continued to rise so that the peak was reached in early 1974. By then the OPEC oil price increase had been implemented. Now an energy shortage was added to the food shortage and Doomsday models that imply economies should shrink rather than grow became even more respectable. Our work commenced amidst this gloomy setting.

Our conjecture at the outset of the study was that by the time any results were in print, the world food crisis would have abated and this prediction has been borne out by subsequent events. Now in the summer of 1977 the U.S. price of wheat has fallen in real terms (1967 dollars) to the same level that it reached in 1932. In our judgment this does not negate the significance of the study, since the cyclical history of the world grain sector suggests that the same issues will arise in the future.

Our focus in the study is on the trade-offs that exist in a multi-country setting. Trade in grains among countries substitutes for supply and inventory changes in particular countries. The model itself is a short run model with a crop year time horizon. The emphasis then is on the structure of the demand for grain in a multi-country world. We attempt to explain the short run changes in flows of grains and prices. The supply of grain is taken to be determined outside the model. This same forecasting structure can be utilized to analyze policy problems as we show in the last two chapters.

We would like to acknowledge support from the Agricultural Experiment Station at North Carolina State University. Many individuals provided assistance, and the encouragement and criticism of Bruce Gardner and D. Gale Johnson were especially useful. Gary Wells and Keith Collins performed as able research assistants, and our typing was done accurately and diligently by Carol Smith.

Some of the material in Chapter 7 is also used in "Devaluation, Foreign Trade Controls, and Domestic Wheat Policy," by Paul R. Johnson, Thomas Grennes and Marie Thursby, *American Journal of Agricultural Economics* 59 (November 1977). The material appears here with the permission of the Journal.

CONTENTS

LIST OF TABLES

1
INTRODUCTION

The purpose of this book is to explain the determinants of grain prices and the pattern of international grain trade. We attempt to explain year-to-year fluctuation in prices and trade flows, so that the analysis emphasizes how the structure of world grain demand responds to predetermined fluctuations in supply. The question of how factor supplies, technology, and climate interact to determine the secular supply of grain is of great importance, but those issues do not lie within the scope of this study. Thus the time horizon for our analysis is the short run.

The immediate motivation for the study was the volatile behavior of world grain trade in the 1970s, which seemed to require an explanation. From the Korean War until 1971 grain prices had followed a steadily declining trend without major fluctuations, but the market situation was suddenly reversed, and by 1973–74 prices spurted to the highest level since World War II. An immediate question was whether this new situation was a permanent or transitory phenomenon. Many explanations for the price increase were offered, and we sought a systematic explanation that was consistent with earlier episodes in grain markets rather than an ad hoc explanation such as a change in climate or the capricious nature of Pacific anchovies. This led us to construct a model based on inherited economic theory.

Subsequent events demonstrated the temporary nature of the price increase as the real wheat price declined until by the middle of 1977 it reached the level it had occupied during the Great Depression. One of the major lessons to emerge from an analysis of world grain trade is the cyclical nature of both economic variables and political concern. Grain production has fluctuated throughout history, and the severity of the problem depends on the response of economic actors and their governments. An ancient institution for alleviating the problems caused by crop fluctuation is international trade. Modern technology applied to

1

communication and transportation could make it easier for international trade to act as a buffer against localized crop shortfalls. However, government policy has often been directed at domestic price stability, and the resulting trade controls have reduced the stabilizing effects of world trade. We will analyze the effects of grain trade policy in terms of our economic model in subsequent chapters.

TYPES OF GRAIN

While our purpose is to analyze world trade in a testing and predicting framework, it should be useful to describe briefly the products we are dealing with. The three commodities we take up specifically are wheat, feed grains, and rice.

Wheat can be classified in several different ways. In some areas, such as the United States and the USSR, wheat is broadly classified as winter wheat and spring wheat. Winter wheat is planted in the fall to be harvested the following summer. Spring wheat is planted in the spring of the year to be harvested later in the summer. This classification of wheat is determined by climate, winter wheat being grown in the more temperate areas of the broad wheat-growing regions, spring wheat being grown in the colder areas. In the Great Plains of the United States the cutoff between winter and spring wheats is roughly the latitude of the South Dakota-Nebraska border. The bulk of Canadian wheat is thus spring wheat grown in the Great Plains.

Another broad classification of wheat is soft and hard. Whether wheat is soft or hard determines its end use, but the determination of where it is grown is again a climatic one. In the United States the soft wheats are grown in the more humid areas of the Midwest and the East, while the hard wheats are grown in the more arid Great Plains. Typically, the soft wheats are used in cakes, pastries, crackers, and similar products, while the hard wheats are the superior bread wheats.

Durum wheat, which is grown in the Dakotas and Canada, is an ultra-hard wheat used in pasta and noodle products. In terms of total world production and trade, durum wheat is a specialty crop. The white wheats are a soft wheat grown in the Pacific Northwest of the United States. Even if we omit durum from consideration, it is clear that wheat is apt to be traded both within and between countries as the uses of the different wheats vary by type. Bakers in the Eastern United States will want the hard western wheats for their bread products, even though local varieties may be in abundance. A region such as Western Europe, which is a large producer of wheat, will want to import U.S. and Canadian hard wheats as their indigenous wheat is largely of the soft variety. The composition of U.S. wheat production and exports abroad is shown in Table 1.1.

TABLE 1.1

Composition of U.S. Wheat Production and Exports, 1975–76

	Production, Million Bushels	Percent	Exports, Million Bushels	Percent
Hard winter	1,053	49.3	581	49.5
Red winter	343	16.1	165	14.1
Hard spring	326	15.3	160	13.6
Durum	123	5.8	52	4.4
White	290	13.6	215	18.3
Total	2,135	100.0	1,173	100.0

Source: U.S. Department of Agriculture, *Wheat Situation* (Washington, D.C.: February 1977).

Historically, wheat and rice have been the main staples in human food. However, wheat also serves as an animal feed. We include the feed component of wheat in all wheat rather than in our feed-grain category. In the developed, Western world, human wheat consumption has been almost steady for a decade. Estimates of the income elasticity for wheat are either zero or negative. Any large swings in annual consumption in those countries will be due to changes in animal use of the grains. The use of wheat for food and feed is shown in Table 1.2 for selected countries for several years.

Feed grains are also far from a homogeneous commodity. They are exactly what the name implies, grains fed to animals that are raised for slaughter or work purposes. For most purposes another internationally used term, coarse grains, is a substitute label. Both terms differentiate other grains from wheat and rice. In the United States feed grains are mainly corn, while in Europe and Canada they are barley for the most part. Feed grains in the United States, then, consist of corn, barley, and grain sorghums. In earlier times oats were also a large component of feed grains, but they have diminished greatly with the reduction in the number of draft animals.

As in the case of types of wheat, feed grain composition is largely a function of climate. Barley is grown in the same areas as wheat. Corn, on the other hand, needs more moisture and warmth than the western and northern wheat areas in the United States can provide. Grain sorghums in the United States compete with wheat in the Southwestern Plains.

Rice is a widely consumed food staple in large areas of Asia and Latin America. Hardly any rice is fed to animals. While rice is an important food, it is

TABLE 1.2

Food and Feed Use of Wheat
in Selected Countries for Selected Years
(1,000 metric tons)

	Average 1959–64	Average 1964–69	1969–70	1970–71	1971–72	1972–73	1973–74	1974–75
Food Use								
United States	13,606	13,964	14,168	14,139	14,315	14,364	14,372	14,288
Canada	1,527	1,624	1,715	1,754	1,776	1,760	1,777	1,902
Australia	1,182	1,220	1,274	1,285	1,276	1,272	1,362	1,389
European Economic Community	26,316	25,806	25,564	24,452	25,797	25,573	25,872	25,525
Feed Use								
United States	911	2,788	5,272	5,089	7,228	5,163	3,818	1,823
Canada	1,387	1,491	2,671	1,880	2,227	2,061	1,834	1,973
Australia	518	572	321	395	534	934	911	1,000
European Economic Community	6,955	8,588	12,124	12,270	11,978	14,157	11,604	12,520

Source: *World Wheat Statistics*, 1974 and 1976.

much less important than wheat or feed grains as an internationally traded commodity. Most rice is consumed in the area in which it is grown.

AN OVERVIEW OF THE WORLD GRAIN ECONOMY

Some summary information on world grain production in selected time periods is presented in Table 1.3. All quantities are in terms of million metric tons. The total world production of grains has been over 1 billion metric tons in the 1970s. This amount of grain is broken down into three components: wheat, coarse grains, and rice. Coarse grains make up approximately half of total world production, wheat approximately 30 percent, and rice 20 percent.

Later, we make six countries endogenous for our analysis of the world wheat economy. Total grain production in these six (United States, Canada, Australia, Argentina European Economic Community [EEC], and Japan) is shown separately in Table 1.3. Of these six the United States is clearly the largest producer of all grains. This is largely the result of the dominant position

TABLE 1.3

World Grain Production: Distribution by Type and Country (million metric tons)

	1960/61– 1962/63 Average	1969/70– 1971/72 Average	1972/73	1973/74	1974/75
World grain	799.2	1,069.2	1,101.4	1,194.1	1,141.8
World wheat	233.2	323.2	339.0	368.8	349.9
World coarse grain	410.1	538.5	559.3	607.3	572.2
World rice	155.9	207.5	213.1	218.0	220.5
U.S. grain	168.2	208.7	227.0	236.1	203.0
Canada grain	22.9	32.4	33.3	34.9	29.8
Australia grain	10.7	14.9	11.0	17.8	17.3
Argentina grain	13.0	19.7	22.8	23.8	19.8
EEC grain	70.2	93.2	102.9	105.5	107.6
Japan grain	15.5	12.7	11.5	11.5	11.7
Subtotal	300.5	381.6	408.5	429.6	389.2
USSR grain	123.3	165.0	157.4	207.5	181.9

Source: U.S. Department of Agriculture, *World Agricultural Situation* (Washington, D.C.: Government Printing Office, June 1975).

TABLE 1.4

World Wheat Production
(thousand metric tons)

Year	United States	Canada	Australia	Argentina	EEC–9	Japan	Subtotal	USSR	World*
1966/67	35,699	22,516	12,700	6,247	30,586	1,024	108,772	100,499	284,245
1967/68	41,433	16,137	7,547	7,320	35,950	970	109,357	77,300	271,543
1968/69	42,899	17,686	14,804	5,740	36,763	1,012	118,904	93,393	305,486
1969/70	39,263	18,623	10,547	7,020	35,703	758	111,914	79,917	285,751
1970/71	36,783	9,022	7,890	4,920	34,807	474	93,896	99,664	287,155
1971/72	44,029	14,413	8,510	5,680	40,058	440	113,130	98,760	319,896
1972/73	42,046	14,514	6,434	7,900	41,375	284	112,553	85,800	310,918
1973/74	46,407	16,460	12,094	6,560	41,393	202	123,116	109,700	340,904
1974/75	48,879	13,295	11,357	5,970	45,388	232	125,121	83,913	323,418
1975/76 (provisional)	58,070	17,100	11,732	8,560	38,112	241	133,815	66,144	313,770

*Excludes China.

Source: World Wheat Statistics, 1976.

6

of the United States in the production of feed grains. The table also singles out the USSR. Of the countries shown, it ranks second to the United States in total grain production.

World wheat production (excluding Communist China) is broken down by country in Table 1.4. The last column in the table shows the variability in world wheat production. One should also note that the ups and downs in world wheat production follow exactly those of the USSR. The output of the other six countries shown, which are subtotaled in the second from last column, shows a more stable behavior through the ten-year period. Thus the Soviet Union, which is by far the largest wheat-producing country in the world, has the most erratic behavior in output. A large part of the land devoted to grain in the USSR is located in areas that are simply quite risky in terms of both moisture and temperature levels. Annual changes in weather in the USSR can impart sharp changes in output and prices for the wheat economy at large. The table also shows that the United States is the second largest wheat producer in the world. The combined countries of the EEC form a region roughly comparable to the United States in wheat production.

TABLE 1.5

Major World Exporters of Wheat
(thousand metric tons)

Country	1959/60– 1963/64 Average	1964/65– 1968/69 Average	1969/70– 1973/74 Average	1974/75
United States	18,359	19,539	23,254	28,325
Canada	10,175	11,839	12,332	11,168
Australia	5,408	6,303	7,310	8,049
Argentina	2,210	3,291	1,951	2,178
EEC-9*	3,558	4,944	5,408	7,193
Subtotal	39,710	46,546	50,255	56,913
Share of United States (percent)	40.5	37.1	40.3	44.7
Share of five (percent)	87.5	88.3	87.8	89.7
USSR	4,449	3,593	4,955	4,000
Sweden	169	272	308	1,054
World	45,367	52,727	57,771	63,429

*Excludes EEC–6 intratrade up to 1971/72 and EEC–9 thereafter.
Source: World Wheat Statistics, 1976.

TABLE 1.6

Major World Importers of Wheat
(thousand metric tons)

Country	1959/60–1963/64 Average	1964/65–1968/69 Average	1969/70–1973/74 Average	1974/75
EEC-9/6[a]	5,044	3,760	4,879	5,343
Japan	2,951	3,914	5,013	5,404
USSR	1,825	3,641	4,844	2,934
China	3,355	4,843	4,557	5,675
India	3,686	5,933	2,306	5,392
Pakistan	1,209	1,483	1,153	1,574
Brazil	2,076	2,432	2,160	1,663
Egypt	1,526	2,215	2,773	3,489
South Korea	518	787	1,714	1,703
Bangladesh[b]				2,057
East Germany	1,415	1,526	1,604	1,555
Poland	1,682	1,462	1,496	1,234
Czechoslovakia	1,189	1,309	1,176	676
World[c]	43,807	52,355	57,665	63,139

[a]EEC–6 prior to 1971/72.
[b]Separate from Pakistan beginning 1971/72.
[c]Excludes China.
Source: World Wheat Statistics, 1976.

Summary statistics for the wheat trading sector are shown in Tables 1.5 and 1.6. The data for exporters are in Table 1.5, while those for importers are shown in Table 1.6. A quick comparison of the two tables shows how much more concentrated exporters are relative to importers. In fact, the U.S. share of world wheat prices has been roughly 40 percent for some time. The major exporters of wheat are the United States, Canada, Australia, and Argentina. These four countries plus the European Economic Community supply over 85 percent of the world's wheat exports. The EEC and USSR appear in Table 1.5 as relatively large exporters, but they also appear in Table 1.6 as relatively large importers. This simultaneous appearance on both sides of the market has implications later for the way we view the grain economy.

The data in Table 1.6 show that the group of importers is more diverse than the group of exporters. While the broad trend over time of imports naturally reflects the same increase as exports, the behavior within particular importing countries reflects more fluctuations in imports than is shown by exporters.

TABLE 1.7

U.S. Wheat Prices, 1913–77*

Crop Year	Current Dollars Per Bushel	1967 Dollars Per Bushel	Crop Year	Current Dollars Per Bushel	1967 Dollars Per Bushel
1913	.88	2.96	1945	1.66	3.08
1914	.94	3.12	1946	1.90	3.25
1915	1.29	4.24	1947	2.60	3.89
1916	1.33	4.07	1948	2.41	3.34
1917	2.30	5.99	1949	2.15	3.01
1918	2.16	4.79	1950	2.23	3.09
1919	2.42	4.67	1951	2.40	3.08
1920	2.46	4.10	1952	2.39	3.01
1921	1.33	2.48	1953	2.24	2.80
1922	1.21	2.41	1954	2.31	2.87
1923	1.11	2.17	1955	2.26	2.82
1924	1.23	2.40	1956	2.22	2.73
1925	1.67	3.18	1957	2.20	2.61
1926	1.50	2.83	1958	2.03	2.34
1927	1.37	2.63	1959	1.98	2.27
1928	1.32	2.57	1960	1.99	2.24
1929	1.18	2.30	1961	2.01	2.24
1930	.90	1.80	1962	NA	—
1931	.61	1.34	1963	2.18	2.38
1932	.49	1.20	1964	1.88	2.02
1933	.72	1.86	1965	1.56	1.65
1934	.93	2.32	1966	1.79	1.84
1935	1.04	2.53	1967	1.67	1.67
1936	1.12	2.70	1968	1.47	1.41
1937	1.20	2.79	1969	1.39	1.27
1938	.78	1.85	1970	1.48	1.27
1939	.76	1.83	1971	1.60	1.32
1940	.87	2.07	1972	2.26	1.80
1941	.99	2.24	1973	4.83	3.63
1942	1.19	2.44	1974	4.29	2.90
1943	1.44	2.78	1977†	2.33	1.30
1944	1.60	3.04			

*Prices refer to No. 2 hard red winter wheat at Kansas City.

†May 23, 1977 quotation.

Source: U.S. Department of Commerce, Bureau of the Census, *Historical Statistics of the United States* (Washington, D.C.: 1975).

WHEAT PRICES

One of our objectives is to construct a model that will explain the behavior of wheat prices in the major trading countries. To provide a perspective for our later discussion, we present data on U.S. wheat prices in Table 1.7. They are wholesale prices at Kansas City for an important variety of wheat (no. 2 hard winter). The time series is by crop years (July-June) and extends from 1913 to the present. (For a discussion of wheat prices in an earlier period see Veblen [1962].) Current dollar prices are presented in the first column and real prices in terms of 1967 dollars appear in the second column. The inflation factor was removed by deflating with the Consumer Price Index.

In the history of U.S. wheat prices for this century, several characteristics stand out. From World War I there is a general downward trend in real wheat prices despite the use of public policy to resist this trend. There are price cycles, especially during periods of major wars. Prices that were around $3.00 per bushel before World War I rose to a peak near $6.00 in 1917 and fell to nearly $2.00 by 1923. Prices were less than $2.00 just before World War II, rose just above $3.00 during the war, and reached their peak at nearly $4.00 in 1947. Since then prices declined steadily for nearly 25 years until the most recent cycle of 1972-75, when they doubled in one year and reached their peak at $3.63 in 1973-74. A complete reversal has occurred since then, and in May 1977 the real wheat price was nearly as low as at any time in this century. The other two periods with comparable low prices are 1969-71 and the trough of the Great Depression in 1932-33.

REFERENCES

International Wheat Council. *World Wheat Statistics*. London: Various issues.

U.S. Department of Agriculture. 1976. *Agricultural Statistics*. Washington, D.C.

U.S. Department of Agriculture. *Wheat Situation*. Washington, D.C.: Various issues.

U.S. Department of Agriculture. 1975. *World Agricultural Situation*. Washington, D.C.: June.

U.S. Department of Commerce, Bureau of the Census. 1975. *Historical Statistics of the United States*. Washington, D.C.

Veblen, Thorstein. 1962. "The Price of Wheat Since 1867." In *Landmarks in Political Economy*, ed. Earl J. Hamilton, Albert Rees, and Harry G. Johnson. Chicago: University of Chicago Press.

2

HISTORICAL PERSPECTIVE ON GRAIN TRADE POLICY

Grain has been an important source of food and drink for thousands of years. Wheat was apparently domesticated as early as 6000 B.C., and early history provides many accounts of grain trade. During its period of prosperity, ancient Rome was actively engaged in importing grain, although Adam Smith reproached the Romans for pursuing a price policy that led them to violate their comparative advantage (Smith 1937, p. 150). Grain plays a prominent role in several Biblical stories. In order to construct his temple, King Solomon exported wheat to acquire cedars from Lebanon. Joseph initiated a grain reserve policy in Egypt and utilized his superior knowledge of the Egyptian weather cycle to stabilize the rate of grain consumption. Grain trade has been important for many centuries, but economic growth combined with a low income elasticity of demand has reduced the share of grain in the average consumer's budget. In spite of this relative decline, wheat continues to be the most important agricultural product that is traded internationally today.

Grain was granted a special status in economic thought by prominent economists such as Adam Smith and Alfred Marshall. Because of the importance of grain in the budgets of workers, Smith chose grain as the numeraire in terms of which real wages were expressed. He stressed "the great and essential difference which nature has established between corn and almost every other sort of good." This difference was that "the nature of things has stamped upon corn a real value which cannot be altered by merely altering its money price" (Smith 1937, p. 482).

Marshall noted the continued importance of grain in working-class budgets in nineteenth-century England and Sweden and the high correlation between grain prices and marriage rates in those two countries (Marshall 1961, pp. 157–58). The diminution of real income brought about by a higher wheat price also inspired Marshall's report of the celebrated Giffen paradox,* in which the bread consumption of the British working class allegedly violated the law of demand (Marshall 1961, pp. 109-19). The income effect of the higher bread price was said to dominate the incentive to substitute cheaper goods for bread.†

The political importance of grain has been acknowledged in political thought and policy. A common expression for fundamental political problems is "bread and butter issues." Socrates considered knowledge of grain to be a necessary condition for political success in ancient Greece. According to Xenophon's account, Socrates' opinion was that "No one was qualified to become a statesman who was entirely ignorant of the problem of wheat" (Hevesy 1940, p. v). In regulating grain trade, governments have developed special institutions such as the variable import levy. The variable levy is an automatic device for separating domestic prices from foreign prices, and it was a key component of the English Corn Laws for more than 300 years, and today it remains a key feature of the Common Agricultural Policy of the European Economic Community. Despite the widespread use of import controls throughout history, variable levies appear to have been used solely for the regulation of grain trade. Haberler (1936, pp. 343-45) cites several European applications of the variable levy in the nineteenth century and they all involved grain.

Our purpose is to provide a systematic explanation of the pattern of grain trade and prices among the major countries of the world. After a survey of some earlier work on trade models, we will develop a formal model and employ the model to analyze the experience since 1960. We take it as self-evident that fluctuations in the weather are a major disturbance to grain markets. In addition our analysis will emphasize the influence of government trade policy on world grain markets. Government policy is in principle more amenable to control than the weather, but in responding to natural shocks it has the potential to dampen cycles or to exacerbate them. History is complicated, but we find much evidence that government trade policy has been a major destabilizing force in world grain markets, especially since 1970. However, before formally analyzing recent trade policy, it is instructive to look at earlier grain policy to obtain some historical perspective. One lesson to be learned from history is that current problems are not unprecedented.

PROVISION POLICY

In studying government policy toward grain, it is useful to employ the taxonomy of Eli Heckscher, which he used in his celebrated work on mercantilism

---

*On the apocryphal nature of the story, see Stigler (1965).

†A recent empirical study of eighteenth century English budgets that contradicts the Giffen case is Koenker (1977).

(Heckscher 1955). Heckscher distinguished between provision or low-price policy and protection or high-price policy. The object of provision policy is to keep grain cheap and readily available within a country ("hunger for goods") by encouraging imports and discouraging exports of grain. An extreme example of provision policy would be unrestricted or even subsidized imports and a ban on grain exports. An extreme example of protection would be a ban on grain imports and unrestricted or even subsidized exports.

Ancient Rome pursued a provision policy that resulted in low domestic prices. Frequent distributions of grain were made gratuitously or at very low prices, and grain imports from conquered provinces were compelled as a tax in kind. For example, Sicilian farmers were required to sell to Rome a specified quantity of wheat at less than the market price, an operation similar to modern marketing boards (Smith 1937). The resulting low price discouraged local wheat production, and Adam Smith criticized the provision policy as a waste of the natural fertility of the Roman soil (Smith 1937).

Provision policy lapsed in Europe after the decline of the Roman Empire, but it returned in the twelfth century, reaching its peak in the fourteenth century (Heckscher 1955, Vol. 2, p. 91). In medieval Europe provision was the general policy as countries sought to increase the availability of grain to domestic consumers.* Grain export restrictions were far more numerous than import restrictions, and when taxes were levied, they were nearly always higher for exports than for imports. In an attempt to keep grain cheap, England prohibited grain exports as early as 1176 (Heckscher 1955, Vol. 2, p. 90). The French provision policy banned grain exports beginning in the fourteenth century and continued export restriction for many years. However, France did not restrict grain imports until 1819 (Heckscher 1955, Vol. 2, p. 92). As mercantilism emerged in Europe at the end of the medieval period, the policy of grain protection replaced provision policy.

Although today agricultural protection prevails in Europe and most high-income countries, a policy of provision with respect to grain and other food persists in many low-income countries that is similar to the old Roman policy (Johnson 1967, ch. 3). The allocative effect of this low-price policy is to promote the expansion of the industrial sector relative to agriculture. Food prices are kept low by price controls, differential tariffs, an overvalued exchange rate, or the acceptance of foreign aid in the form of food. Exports are discouraged by comparable devices such as quantitative restrictions or an unfavorable exchange rate. The provisionist policies of low-income countries complement the protection of high-income countries, and the net effect is to alter the location of world grain production toward high-income countries. It is not

---

*An exception to the European provision policy was Prussia of Frederick William I, which attempted to protect local producers with a death penalty for the crime of consuming foreign corn (Heckscher 1955, Vol. 2, p. 93).

entirely clear why agricultural price policy ought to be systematically related to the income of a country, although Engel's Law might provide a hint, since food is relatively more important to consumers in low-income countries.*

PROTECTION POLICY

England was the first European country to replace provision with a policy of protection. An explicit and continuous policy of protection for grain began after the 1688 Revolution with the introduction of the export bounty and lasted until the repeal of the Corn Laws in 1846. However, there were traces of protectionism as early as the fifteenth century, and because of this some writers date the Corn Laws from 1463 (Haberler 1936, pp. 343-45). Prior to that time grain imports were welcome in England, but beginning in 1463 grain imports were banned whenever the domestic price fell below a specified target level (Heckscher 1955, Vol. 2, pp. 143-44). Interestingly, England moved from an extreme policy of provision to an extreme policy of protection in a short period without an intermediate stage of laissez-faire grain policy. This displeased Adam Smith who devoted an entire chapter of *Wealth of Nations* to the pernicious effects of export bounties. The bounty was a discontinuous device since it was paid only when domestic prices were below a target level, and at that point an abrupt change occurred as the bounty ceased and an export embargo was imposed (Heckscher 1955, Vol. 2, pp. 143-44). The bounty was extremely unpopular among consumer groups, and in some years of small harvests rioting in the cities led to suspension of the bounty. Bounties were defended on the mercantilist grounds that they led to a favorable trade balance and attracted gold to the nation.

Just as England had earlier reversed its policy from extreme provision to extreme protection, the repeal of the Corn Laws brought on another major reversal and England soon became a major grain importer. They became the major customer of the United States, buying half of the wheat exported from the United States during the period 1870-1914 (Rothstein 1964, p. 292). After its Civil War, the United States became a major world exporter of grain, and rapid expansion of production led Thorstein Veblen to describe the decade 1873-82 as "the most remarkable period that has been seen in American wheat growing" (Veblen 1962, p. 14). Expansion to western lands, extension of the railroad, and reduction in ocean shipping costs due to the steamship made U.S. wheat much more competitive in European markets after 1870. The cost of

---

*Harry Johnson (1973) suggests that there is an unjustified concern about a backward-bending labor supply curve for agriculture in low income countries.

shipping U.S. wheat to Liverpool in 1900 fell to one-third of the cost of the same trip in 1870 (North 1974, pp. 132–33). During this period the United States displaced Russia as the major grain exporter to Western Europe. Lower inland transport costs and lower ocean shipping costs also contributed to the emergence of Canada, Australia, and Argentina in the 1890s as major exporters (Malenbaum 1953, ch. 9). England responded to these new competitive forces by increasing imports, but the continental response, beginning in 1881, was a wave of protectionism that has continued to the present.

The United States pursued a largely laissez-faire grain policy until World War I. During the English colonial period and up to the Civil War the United States was a minor grain exporter, and in the latter half of the century they became a major world exporter. A U.S. grain tariff did exist, but it "had no economic effect except in isolated cases along the Canadian border" (Taussig 1923, ch. 10). Export controls are circumscribed by the constitutional ban on export taxes, but this does not preclude quantitative restrictions. A combination of World War I damage and price controls led to a worldwide food shortage, and the United States responded by imposing export controls on grain. Export quotas have also been employed as part of the several international wheat agreements with which the United States has been associated since 1933. Recent uses of quotas have been the soybean embargo of 1974 and the brief embargo on wheat exports to the USSR in 1975, prior to the U.S.-USSR five-year grain agreement of 1976.

Governments of the major grain-producing countries became actively involved in fixing domestic grain prices during the Great Depression years. Prices were depressed well below their historical average, and the object of policy was to assist producers by raising prices and insuring some acceptable minimum price. Since these target domestic prices were usually incompatible with world prices, they required the use of trade controls that separated domestic and world markets (Johnson 1950, chs. 1–2). The protectionism that was born in the 1930s continues to dominate grain trade policy in the high-income countries to the present day. Many state trading agencies such as the Canadian Wheat Board were established in the 1930s, and they have been able to implement de facto taxes and quantitative trade controls in a manner that is less conspicuous than in economies that permit private trade. For example, a state importing agency can quietly increase the spread between its domestic selling price to millers and the c.i.f. (cost, insurance, and freight) import price. Similarly, state agencies have subsidized exports by selling abroad at a price below the domestic selling price to millers.

Since World War II, grain exports have been subsidized at various times by all the major exporters in a manner that is reminiscent of the English Corn Laws. After the passage of Public Law (PL) 480 in 1954, the United States sent large quantities of food aid to low-income countries. This program reached its peak in the 1960s when the majority of U.S. grain exports were associated with

PL 480. In addition to food aid the United States subsidized commercial grain exports at a rate varying with the spread between the domestic support price and the world price. The subsidy was suspended in 1972 following the infamous "great grain robbery" by the Soviet Union in the same year, but the abundance of grain in 1977 may soon revive the practice. Protectionist grain policies of high-income countries have met little resistance from low-income countries that have been content to follow policies of provision for agriculture while protecting the manufacturing sector. A problem for importers is that the rate of subsidy has been highly variable due to both political and natural disturbances.

In addition to national protection policies, there has been a continuous collective effort to raise grain prices since 1930 (Hadwiger 1970, p. 70). The International Wheat Agreement of 1933 was the first of a series of formal agreements, and the effort continues today under the auspices of the International Wheat Council in London. The 1933 agreement attempted to raise world prices by assigning export quotas to members, but it was violated within the first year after the signing (Malenbaum 1953, ch. 11). The agreements have not been noticeably successful except to the extent that their goals coincided with the domestic goals of the United States and Canada (McCalla 1966). However, the recent success of the Organization of Petroleum Exporting Countries' cartel has revived interest in commodity agreements, and this interest has been reinforced by the recent abundance of wheat in the world.

Another protectionist force in the richer countries has been the Common Agricultural Policy of the European Economic Community. The original union of six countries was formed in 1957 and it was the largest wheat importer in the world. The admission of the United Kingdom in 1973 significantly increased the importance of EEC grain import policy. Domestic prices have generally been fixed well above world prices by a variable import levy and export subsidy. Because of the market power the EEC countries possess as a buyer of wheat, their trade policy has important implications for grain prices all over the world.

INSULATING TRADE POLICIES

Although recent policy in high-income countries has been primarily protectionist, most governments have at times modified their policies to insulate the domestic market from major changes in foreign prices. Protection refers to the differential between domestic and foreign prices, and insulation refers to changes in the differential caused by changes in the foreign price. This differential can only be changed by compensating changes in trade controls. If a government seeks a target domestic price for grain, then falling world prices would require a higher tariff or export subsidy and rising world prices would require a lower tariff or higher export tax. Thus, protection and insulation are policies that are sometimes compatible and sometimes conflicting. When world prices are falling (rising), insulation requires a greater (lesser) degree of protection. Another characteristic of insulating policies is that some countries can insulate their markets from foreign disturbances, but all countries cannot do this simultaneously if the world market is to clear. This implies that some countries can achieve greater price stability only at the expense of their trading partners. This clearly occurred in 1973-74 when the United States was the only major trading country to refrain from insulating policies. As a result, U.S. domestic grain prices rose much more than they otherwise would have.* However, Americans were collectively compensated for accepting greater price instability, since a higher price and a larger volume of grain exports imply a higher national income.

Insulating trade policies interfere with the price stabilizing function of international trade. Because export demand is more elastic than domestic demand, trade reduces the price change that would result from a given change in domestic supply. Alternatively, prices can be stabilized by compensating inventory fluctuation. When domestic production declines, consumption and price can be stabilized either by an increase in imports or by inventory decumulation. Since trade and inventories perform a common function, trade can be used as a device for economizing on costly inventory holding. Since world production fluctuates less than national production because small yields in some countries tend to be compensated by large yields in other countries, international trade permits the world to stabilize prices with smaller inventories than it would otherwise need (Malenbaum 1953, pp. 91-93). Trade has the potential to substitute for inventories as a price stabilizer, but this potential will not be realized if international trade controls are imposed. Just as Bastiat conceived of tariffs as "negative railroads," one can conceive of insulating trade policies as "negative inventories," since they reduce the amount of price stabilization that a given level of reserves can bring about. This implies that one cannot specify the optimal level of grain reserves in the world without simultaneously specifying the set of trade controls that will prevail. Current international negotiations ignore this relationship by carrying out separate and independent negotiations for trade liberalization and world grain reserves.

Insulating trade policies are not a recent invention, but their application has become more systematic in recent years. The English Corn Laws were primarily a protectionist policy, but the bounty was suspended during years of extremely high prices. Europe's protectionist response to U.S. export expansion in the 1880s was an insulating policy (Tracy 1964, ch. 2). The tariff war of the 1930s was an extreme case of the major grain-trading countries trying to insulate their domestic markets from external conditions. The United States passed the

---

*See Chapter 8 for the details of this effect.

Smoot-Hawley tariff of 1930, the highest in its history, and Europe responded
with import quotas, milling quotas, and tariffs of more than 100 percent.

Most insulating trade policies have been discretionary, but they can be
made automatic by letting trade controls vary so as to achieve a fixed target
domestic price that is independent of the foreign price. The English Corn Laws
contained some of this automaticity as early as 1463 for both tariffs and export
subsidies (Haberler 1936, p. 343). For some reason variable levies have been
applied exclusively to grain trade (Haberler 1936, p. 344) and, ironically, the
levy whose purpose is to stabilize prices has been criticized by both Marshall and
Haberler (p. 344) for destabilizing prices. Marshall complained that England's
"perverse mixture of prohibitions and sliding scales rendered it an act of gamb-
ling rather than of sober business to grow wheat" (Marshall 1926, p. 380). The
important current case of automatic insulation is the variable grain levy of the
EEC. A domestic target price is chosen, and the tariff is defined to be whatever
variable amount is necessary to achieve the domestic target. Thus, the import
demand curve for grain becomes perfectly inelastic as the change in the tariff
compensates for any change in the import price. Recently the levy has changed
from more than $2 per bushel in 1971-72 to zero in 1974 to more than $3 per
bushel in 1977. The EEC variable levy is important to world grain trade because
it is automatic, it insulates one of the major grain markets, and the magnitude
of tariff changes has been large.

When world grain prices reached their historical peak in 1973-74, most
major trading countries pursued insulating trade policies. The EEC levy automatically fell to zero, export subsidies were eliminated, and exports to certain
countries were restricted. The Japan Food Agency abandoned its traditional
tariff and subsidized imports by buying at the world price and reselling to
domestic millers at a loss. Argentina imposed a grain embargo, Canada and
Australia taxed exports through the discriminatory pricing policies of their
wheat boards. They sold to domestic millers at far below their selling price to
exporters, the difference constituting an effective export tax. The net effect of
these and other insulating policies was to increase import demand, decrease
export supply, and create a greater excess demand in the remaining markets. The
United States was the major residual market, and because it remained relatively
open, it absorbed most of the adjustment that was avoided by other nations. As
a result domestic prices and the volume of grain exports increased much more in
the United States in 1973-74 than they otherwise would have. Since then world
prices have fallen to normal levels and importing countries have abandoned
subsidies and returned to tariffs. Exporters have abandoned taxes and quantitative restrictions, and they are again promoting sales. Export promotion has gone
so far that U.S. and Canadian officials have openly discussed the need to agree
on a minimum export price.

A discussion of world grain policy is seriously incomplete if it fails to mention the Soviet Union.* The USSR is a major component of the world market and a major source of instability. In the nineteenth century it was the most important source of Western Europe's grain imports. It continues to be a net exporter in certain years, but in other years it has been the world's largest grain importer. The USSR is the world's largest wheat producer, but the salient feature of Soviet production and imports is their instability. In 1972-73 the Soviet Union increased its wheat imports by 11 million tons and the next year they reduced imports by roughly the same amount. It has been estimated that Soviet wheat imports accounted for 80 percent of the variability of world wheat imports in recent years (Mackie 1974). Much of the variability of imports is attributable to changes in production, but Soviet import policy is an additional source of uncertainty. Because Soviet authorities have not permitted imports to respond systematically to crop shortfalls, a difficult forecasting problem has been made even more complicated. The U.S. government has been concerned about the possible disruptive effect of the USSR on the world market, and their attempt to reduce uncertainty with respect to Soviet grain purchases was formalized in the five-year grain agreement of 1976. The agreement specified a permissible range (6-8 million metric tons of corn and wheat) of grain imports per year at prices currently prevailing in the market.

REFERENCES

Haberler, Gottfried. 1936. *The Theory of International Trade.* New York: Macmillan.

Hadwiger, Don. 1970. *Federal Wheat Commodity Programs.* Ames: Iowa State Press.

Heckscher, Eli F. 1955. *Mercantilism.* Vols. 1-2, rev. 2d ed. London: George Allen and Unwin.

Hevesy, Paul de. 1940. *World Wheat Planning and Economic Planning in General.* London: Oxford University Press.

Johnson, D. Gale. 1950. *Trade and Agriculture: A Study of Inconsistent Policies.* New York: Wiley.

——. 1977. *The Soviet Impact on World Grain Trade.* New York: British-North American Committee.

*For a more complete discussion of the Soviet Union see D. Gale Johnson (1977).

Johnson, Harry G. 1967. *Economic Policies Toward Less Developed Countries.* Washington, D.C.: Brookings Institution.

———. 1973. *The Theory of Income Distribution.* London: Gray-Mills.

Koenker, Roger. 1977. "Was Bread Giffen? The Demand for Food in England Circa 1790." *The Review of Economics and Statistics* 59 (May) 225–29.

McCalla, Alex. 1966. "A Duopoly Model of World Wheat Pricing." *Journal of Farm Economics* 48 (August): 711–27.

Mackie, Arthur. 1974. "International Dimension of Agricultural Prices." *Southern Journal of Agricultural Economics* 6 (July): 11–23.

Malenbaum, Wilfred. 1953. *The World Wheat Economy.* Cambridge, Mass.: Harvard University Press.

Marshall, Alfred. 1926. *Official Papers.* London: Macmillan.

Marshall, Alfred. 1961. *Principles of Economics.* 8th ed. London: Macmillan.

North, Douglas. 1974. *Growth and Welfare in the American Past.* 2d ed. Englewood Cliffs, N.J.: Prentice-Hall.

Rothstein, Morton. 1964. "America in the International Rivalry for the British Wheat Market, 1860–1914." In *United States Economic History: Selected Readings*, ed. Harry N. Scheiber. New York: Knopf.

Smith, Adam. 1937. *Wealth of Nations.* New York: Modern Library.

Stigler, George J. 1965. "Notes on the History of the Giffen Paradox." In Stigler, *Essays in the History of Economics.* Chicago: University of Chicago Press.

Taussig, Frank. 1923. *The Tariff History of the United States.* 7th ed. New York: G. P. Putnam's Sons.

Tracy, Michael. 1964. *Agriculture in Western Europe.* New York: Praeger.

Veblen, Thorstein. 1962. "The Price of Wheat Since 1867." In *Landmarks in Political Economy*, ed. Earl J. Hamilton, Albert Rees, and Harry G. Johnson. Chicago: University of Chicago Press.

3
ALTERNATIVE
MODELS OF WORLD
GRAIN TRADE

Conceptually, the problem of developing a model to forecast trade flows of commodities is straightforward, but practically the problem is awesome. This state of affairs is quite normal in economics. One can easily think of demand and supply functions for each good in the economy, and the quantities in each of these functions are related to each price. In analyzing the real world, however, this model is of little use since the numbers of goods and actors are huge. We are faced here with the same kind of problem. Even for one good if there are n regions there are n^2 possible flows of a good. The basic problem for any economic analysis is to abstract from the real world with some limited amount of information about that world. The test of any such model is how well it predicts. That is, one confronts the model with new data and asks the question of how accurate are the predictions in terms of agreement with events or in comparison with alternative models.

In reviewing the models capable of predicting commodity trade flows, one can think of a spectrum of models in terms of the restrictions placed on them. These restrictions come from economic theory and the functional specification of the model. In this view the extremes are spatial equilibrium models and systems dynamics models. Our limited review of systems dynamics indicates that users of these models impose fewer restrictions from economic theory than users of other models. On the other hand, the spatial equilibrium models appear to us to be the most restrictive. They impose the constraint of one homogeneous good with a very restrictive transport cost minimizing market clearing mechanism.

In between these two cases are a host of alternative models. Among these are (1) straightforward estimation of reduced form equations from a structure that includes import and export behavior, (2) an allocative system for distributing imports among various suppliers, and (3) a class of models that distinguishes goods by place of production. All of these models share the attribute that they try to capture behavior in the actual importing and exporting of goods. As indicated below, importing countries may not always buy from the current least-cost source because of lags in behavior, contractual obligations, and other reasons. Forecasting, then, should be sought from models that allow this kind of behavior to enter.

From this array of alternatives we have utilized the model that distinguishes goods by place of production. This class of models stems largely from the work of Armington (1969a, 1969b, 1970a, 1970b, 1973) and has been used by the International Monetary Fund (IMF) and by Branson (1972). The basic proposition of this kind of model is that an importer may not consider wheat, for instance, that comes from the United States and Australia to be identical products. Previous application of this type of model has been for fairly broad classes of products, where the distinction of goods by place of production accords well with one's intuition. That this is a sensible distinction for agricultural products also can be justified.

One of the authors has previously examined this question for several agricultural commodities (Johnson 1971). The problem there was to estimate demand elasticities from the elasticity of substitution in various markets. The statistical estimates were such that one would clearly accept that even U.S. and Canadian wheat were not perfect substitutes. Second, even a casual observation of the range of prices suggests that some attention is being paid to the place of origin of a commodity. Thus, whether it is quality of the product, institutional arrangements, or whatever, short-run decisions appear to be based on things other than transport costs. It appears sensible to us to use a model that can capture some of this behavior in a systematic way.

THE APPLICATION OF SPATIAL MODELS

This section will survey some of the major efforts to employ spatial models to study world trade in wheat, feed grains, and rice. Some of the major shortcomings of such models will be considered, and attempts to modify the models to conform more closely with empirical reality will be discussed.

The theoretical foundation of spatial models was developed by Samuelson (1952). The object of such models is to select prices, quantities, and a pattern of trade that maximized "net social payoff," which is defined as the sum of consumer and producer surplus net of transportation costs. For forecasting purposes, spatial models are a device for employing maximization techniques to solve nonnormative problems (what will trade flows be tomorrow?) by assuming that actors behave as if they attempt to maximize net social payoff. The product being studied is assumed to be homogeneous so that consumers are indifferent about the source of their purchase, and they select sellers solely on the basis of price, including transport costs. Because homogeneity of the product is crucial

89002

to spatial models, most applications have involved narrowly defined products, especially in agriculture and natural resources, rather than broad, heterogeneous aggregates (Schmitz 1968). A recent volume by Judge and Takayama (1973) contains applications to agricultural problems and a paper by Kennedy (1974) employs spatial techniques to construct a model of the world petroleum market.

The basic approach of all the spatial equilibrium models is to divide the world into regions and estimate separate supply and demand (usually linear) equations for each region. Geographical centers of production and consumption are selected for each region, and transport costs between these points are estimated. An equilibrium set of prices, quantities, and trade flows is generated so as to minimize the cost of transporting goods. The characteristic feature of the model is that trade flows are predicted without directly incorporating empirical data on exports and imports of wheat.

Spatial Studies of the Wheat Market

A study by Schmitz and Bawden (1973) divides the world into 15 regions. Eleven are endogenous to the model: United States, Canada, Australia, Argentina, Japan, United Kingdom, Germany, France, Italy, Netherlands, and Belgium-Luxembourg. For each of these regions the model determines price, consumption, production, and trade flows. The rest of the world is divided into Other America, Other Europe, Other Asia and Africa, and the net imports of each of these regions is taken as exogenous, although the model does determine the distribution of their imports among suppliers.

Demand and supply equations are estimated for each of the 11 regions using data from 1959-66. A geographical center of production and consumption for each region is specified, and transport costs between these centers are estimated. Values of the exogenous variables (for example, per capita income, USSR net imports) are projected to 1980, and the model generates forecasts for the 1980 levels of all the endogenous variables. The model predicts demand for countries comprising 22 percent of world consumption and supply for countries comprising 36 percent of world production. It would be informative to compare the minimum transport cost trade matrix which the model generated for the 1960s with the observed world trading pattern for that period. Unfortunately, such a comparison is not presented by Schmitz and Bawden, and this makes it more difficult to judge the reliability of the trade forecast for 1980. The effects of weather changes, tariff changes, the Green Revolution, and so on, are considered by altering the values of the exogenous variable. The major conclusion is that it is very likely that the price of wheat will be lower in 1980 than the minimum prices negotiated by the International Cereals Agreement of 1967 ($1.68-$1.95 per bushel in 1967 prices). Notice that the actual price of U.S. wheat (export price at Gulf ports for no. 2 Hard, red, winter 13 percent) was

$4.85 in 1973-74 and $4.64 in 1974-75 in current dollars or $3.28 and $2.88, respectively, in 1967 dollars. The May 1977 price of wheat is $2.50 in current dollars or $1.30 in 1967 dollars.

A USDA study by Rojko et al. (1971) employed a spatial model to project world grain trade for 1980. They included wheat, coarse grains, and rice in the study and divided the world into 22 regions. For each region a separate demand and supply equation was estimated and projections for each of the $(22)^2 = 484$ possible trade flows were made.

The study was particularly concerned about the role of developing countries, and the effect of various rates of growth in their agricultural productivity were considered. In addition, the model analyzed the effects of various import and export policies of developed countries. Instead of projecting prices for 1980, the study projects the world excess supply that would exist in 1980 at 1964-66 prices. The precise results depend on the assumed values of exogenous variables, but most policy combinations considered result in a world wheat surplus by 1980. The authors point out the similarity between their projections and 1974 studies by the U.S. Department of Agriculture (USDA) and the UN Food and Agriculture Organization (FAO), and they also correspond closely to the results of a recent study by Blakeslee, Heady, and Framingham (1973).

The structure of the model is very similar to the Schmitz-Bawden wheat model. The USDA study incorporates feed grains and rice and divides the world more finely. The major difference, however, is that they make a greater effort to diversify trade flows by adding direct restraints that, for example, require that 20 percent of Japanese wheat imports come from Australia, 30 percent from Canada, and 50 percent from the United States, regardless of transport costs. The authors concede that restraints are imposed on the model because actual trade flows do not minimize transport costs.* The numerical restraints they impose are based on historical trade flows. This technique of implicitly introducing historical trade data differs from the models of Armington (1969a, 1969b, 1970a, 1970b, 1973) and Truman-Resnick (1973) in which historical trade shares, modified for price and income changes, are the major determinant of future trade flows.

Empirical Verification

The following comments are directed at the studies mentioned above, but they are applicable with some modification to spatial models in general.

---

*A similar technique is used by Kost (1975) in his model of intra-EEC trade in grains. The restraints he imposes are derived from historical trade flow data.

If one's objective is to predict prices, production, consumption, and trade flows in the world wheat economy, one can construct a spatial model that generates a trade matrix that minimizes the cost of transporting wheat from producers to consumers. One can then compare the flows generated by the model with actual flows, and deviations of actual from predicted values can be interpreted as forecasting errors. An alternative normative interpretation is that the deviations measure the inefficiency of the actual trade flows relative to the "optimal" flows generated by the model (see Wallace 1963, Dean and Collins 1966). However, the normative question of whether or not the actual wheat trade flows are efficient need not concern us in the present investigation.

The first problem is the extent to which exporters concentrate their sales in a small number of markets. Spatial models seem to have an inherent bias toward specialization that results from the objective of minimizing transport costs. For example, one projection of the Schmitz-Bawden model has the United States sending all of its wheat exports to Asia (excluding Japan) whereas, historically, U.S. exports have been much more diversified. The implication of this bias is that the trade matrix predicted by a spatial model will have many more zero entries than an actual trade matrix. This also creates errors in the predicted direction of trade, since the model predicts that countries will buy primarily from the nearest exporter. However, in 1972-73 the biggest wheat customers of the United States were Japan, Korea, Brazil, and Germany. All of them have closer neighbors (Australia, Argentina, and France) who are major exporters, yet they bought as much wheat or more from the United States (United Nations 1974).

This bias stems from the logic of spatial models. That is, they are designed to predict trade flows for a homogeneous good. If a good is homogeneous, then interregional price differences for the good result only from transport costs and trade barriers. In the case of wheat, this means that at a common consumption point, such as Rotterdam, U.S. and Canadian wheat should sell for the same price; and producer prices for those countries' wheat should differ only by transport costs and taxes. In that case a spatial equilibrium model is a reasonable framework in which to study trade flows in the good. Thus if wheat produced by the United States and Canada are perfect substitutes in consumption, we would expect those models to predict multilateral trade flows and prices as well as any alternative model. If, however, different types of wheat are imperfect substitutes in consumption, then we might expect a spatial model to predict fewer and different trades occurring than would actually occur. For example, countries preferring wheat from a particular source may import that type of wheat even if transport costs are higher than for a less preferred type of wheat. Also, if the Japanese prefer to import wheat from a number of sources, then a model that minimizes transport costs would tend to predict Japanese imports from fewer sources than would be the case. As pointed out in an earlier section, this problem can be solved by placing additional constraints on the optimization problem. That technique only partially solves the problem inherent in using a spatial equilibrium model where the good is not perfectly homogeneous, because in that case cross-hauling is a plausible phenomenon. Cross-hauling is precluded in spatial equilibrium models, and by its exclusion the number of multilateral trade flows is limited to 2n - 1, where n is the number of potential exporters and importers of the good. This shortcoming is often expressed by the statement that the model provides information about net trade flows but not about gross flows. A related shortcoming of the model is that adjustments in the trade matrix to exogenous shocks are large and abrupt rather than smooth and continuous. Thus, a small change in transport costs or tariffs may immediately reduce a country's exports to a particular market from a large volume to zero.

To some extent the above problem stems from the aggregation of data for products and geographical regions. The availability of data requires that many different varieties of wheat and wheat flour be treated as a single aggregate. This aggregate conceals differences in variety and quality and seasonality, which might readily explain cross-hauling, buying from more distant sources, or diversification of imports and exports. This problem is common to all models that deal with wheat but it is more serious for spatial models because they do not employ historical trade data that would incorporate some of these features.

A further problem with spatial models is the difficulty of incorporating time lags and institutional arrangements. For example, A may import from B today to satisfy a previously arranged contract even though B is no longer the cheapest source. Similarly, A may import from C because cultural ties provide a cheap flow of information, and this cost advantage may outweigh a transport cost disadvantage. Presumably, the variable that spatial models seek to measure is some index of marketing costs, and transportation is merely one of its components. Policy measures that promote (for example, export subsidies) trade or discourage trade (for example, tariffs) present the same kind of problem, but if the policy is quantifiable, spatial models can deal with them.

The above criticism applies primarily to the trade flow portion of the model rather than the price and production predictions. The latter are determined by the same supply and demand framework employed by many other kinds of models. If the trade analysis is the weaker part of the model, then the trade flow predictions ought to be poorer than the price predictions, and there is some evidence that this is the case (Bjarnason 1967).

Modifications of Spatial Models

An extreme form of a spatial model would determine trade flows solely by minimizing transport cost. Nearly everyone who has employed spatial models concedes that the world does not behave this way, and various suggestions to alter the objective function have been proposed. The most obvious adjustment is to incorporate trade barriers, and these techniques are ably summarized by Bawden (1966) and Dean and Collins (1966).

A second modification is to impose quantitative restrictions that force trade flows in certain directions and quantities and forbid other flows. The USDA studies by Rojko et al. and by Kost (1975) employ these restrictions extensively. This appears to be an awkward and somewhat arbitrary way of introducing historical trade behavior. Additionally, as Kost notes, there are limits to the number of restrictions one can impose on the flows. For example, in a three-region model, there are six possible interregional flows, but since the model predicts only net flows, the flow from 1 to 2 is equal to the flow from 2 to 1 with opposite sign. Thus, there are only three independent flows, and once these have been restricted, there is nothing left for the transport model to determine.

In spite of the shortcomings mentioned above, spatial models possess many desirable properties for long-run forecasting purposes, and attempts to modify them to overcome the difficulties encountered in their use for short-run forecasting may prove to be fruitful. However, in our judgment, most of these problems are better dealt with by constructing a model that directly incorporates historical trade behavior. The essence of spatial wheat models is that consumers view wheat from all exporters as perfect substitutes, but data on market prices frequently contradict that proposition. For example, in September 1974 in Rotterdam, Canadian and U.S. wheat sold for the same price, but four months earlier in the same city, Canadian wheat sold at a dollar premium over U.S. wheat (USDA 1974). For forecasting purposes one need not be able to explain why price differences exist or why they change, but it is essential that the information conveyed by these prices and observed trade patterns be incorporated into one's forecasting model. In our judgment, this is accomplished more easily by abandoning the spatial framework.

SYSTEMS DYNAMICS MODELS

An alternative view of the world that has been used for forecasting problems is that originating in industrial engineering, sometimes called systems dynamics. The best-known applications have been to global problems, for example, Jay W. Forrester's (1971) *World Dynamics* and Donella Meadows et al.'s (1972) *The Limits to Growth*.

We have not made an extensive study of these forecasting models because they have been subjected to detailed criticism elsewhere (Solow 1972; Nordhaus 1973). For our current purposes it will be sufficient to list some of the well-known shortcomings of such models.

The basic technique involves computer simulation, and criticism has been directed at both model construction and empirical validation. The formal relationships among the variables are not based on established economic theory, and the perspective is so remote from economics as to ignore such a fundamental concept as a production function. One of the dangers of constructing an ad hoc model rather than one based on an established theory is that the model builder can "assume his conclusions." For example, if one is interested in the price of wheat in 1980, there exists some set of explanatory variables and parameter values that will generate growth rates of demand and supply that will yield a price of $100 per bushel and others that will yield a price of $.50 per bushel. Obviously, these two prices have vastly different implications so that it would seem important to place restrictions on the choice of explanatory variables and the parameter values that are more objective than the model builder's intuition.

A related shortcoming of the Forrester and Meadows models is the absence of a well-functioning price mechanism that registers and reacts to scarcity. Both theory and facts indicate that shortages are self-correcting because higher prices induce consumers and producers to switch to exisitng substitutes and to search for new ones. Models that lack price adjustment are more likely to yield extreme forecasts.

The most fundamental weakness of Forrester and Meadows is the failure to base their equations on empirical data. For this reason Nordhaus has described Forrester's work as "measurement without data." In *World Dynamics* "not a single relationship or variable is drawn from actual data or empirical studies" (Nordhaus 1973). Not only are parameters not based on detailed statistical estimation, but there is no clear standard of the model's goodness of fit. This is particularly important in the case of *World Dynamics* since the model's main implication (world standard of living will peak in 1990 and decline thereafter) is quite sensitive to the model specification of population growth, technical change, and input substitutability (Nordhaus 1973, p. 1178 ff.).

It appears that the major virtue of systems dynamics is its capacity to deal with time lags by using difference or differential equations. However, such techniques also have a long history in econometrics and it is possible to include such behavior in our model.

REVIEW OF REDUCED-FORM MODELS

There are no particular studies of this genre that we know of to give us guidance in this area. We regard such models as potential alternatives to what we have employed.

The reduced-form terminology comes from econometrics. Consider a simple market for a good such as wheat.

$$q = f^1(P, I, X) \qquad\qquad\qquad 1a$$

$$q = f^2(P, W, Z) \qquad\qquad\qquad 1b$$

1a is a demand equation and 1b is a supply equation. Each of these relates a flow of a good to its price and other variables. In the case of demand these variables include specifically income, and in the case of supply, specifically weather. Equations 1a and 1b are the structure. Behavior on both sides of the market is what one would like to know. In this case, it is easy to think of price and quantity as being simultaneously determined, and the other variables given from outside the market under consideration. Such a system can be solved for price and quantity as endogenous variables in terms of the other variables and the parameters that relate these variables to P and q.

$$q = g^1 (I, X, W, Z) \qquad\qquad\qquad 2a$$

$$P = g^2 (I, X, W, Z) \qquad\qquad\qquad 2b$$

Here, the two endogenous variables are now functions of all the outside variables in the system.

There are certain advantages to looking at equations 2a and b rather than 1a and b. If one wants to predict the behavior of the endogenous variables when the system is shocked, the initial impact is given by the coefficients on, say, W in 2a and 2b. A forecast of an endogenous variable may thus be made without the structure being exactly specified. One only needs to know what variables are in the structure and the reduced-form coefficients on the appropriate values.

A second desirable aspect of looking at reduced forms is that each reduced-form equation is amenable to ordinary least-squares regression techniques for estimating coefficients. Thus direct estimates of responses can be easily gotten.*

Another advantage of looking at reduced forms is that lagged behavior can be easily incorporated. Subject to the caveat of the previous footnote, some dynamic behavior can be estimated without specifying exactly such behavior in the structure.

Our point of view probably is best stated that looking at reduced-form specifications of behavior in trade flows may be the best alternative to the models that distinguish products by place of production. That is, trade behavior can be estimated from historical data directly by regression techniques. Such behavior would then serve for future forecasting.

The basic structure would be the excess demand and supply functions for a commodity such as wheat. That is, the excess supply of an exporter like the United States is made up of components from domestic demand and supply, and

---

*Ordinary least-squares estimates of this kind ignore the structure, and are thus not the best estimates one can get. The advantage alleged here only refers to the ease of securing estimates and not in the statistical properties of the estimators.

the demand facing the United States is then made up of the excess demand functions of the importers. It is possible to think of estimating the reduced forms for this structure for all the trading regions. The endogenous variables would be the flows between regions and the price in each region, these endogenous variables would then be regressed on the exogenous variables plus any policy variables and shifters that might be specified.

TRADE MODELS FOR DIFFERENTIATED PRODUCTS

Models in which consumers distinguish products by place of production describe trade flows for nonhomogeneous goods. By nonhomogeneous we mean that the good produced by one country is an imperfect substitute for the same good produced in another country. When this is the case, the good produced by a particular country typically is called a product (Armington 1969a). In our case, wheat produced in the United States would be called a product. It would be distinguished from other goods (rice, feed grains) because it is a type of wheat and from other types of wheat (Canadian, Argentinean) because it is an imperfect substitute for them. U.S. wheat may be viewed differently by consumers than Argentinean wheat because of characteristics intrinsic or extrinsic to the products themselves. Several such cases can be distinguished.

First, the good might be "intrinsically heterogeneous." That is, differences in quality may be observed across producers, or data for the good may exist only for an aggregate of varieties of the good. In the case of manufactures, it could easily be argued that producers tried to differentiate their products and that the aggregate of manufactures would differ in composition across countries. The same arguments apply to primary commodities since varieties and quality are likely to vary by supplier. In particular for agricultural commodities, such as wheat, different varieties are suited for growing in different geographical areas, so that variety composition of wheat exports is likely to vary by country. Given that wheat varieties are not perfect substitutes in producing bread, pastries, and so on, importers are likely to differentiate their demands. Even for trade of one variety, data would be an aggregate of qualities that may vary by country.

Second, even if a good is intrinsically homogeneous, products may be viewed differently by importers because of "national factors." To the extent that trading is state trading one would expect products supplied by political allies to be viewed differently than others. This factor would be operative both on the export and import side of the market. Exporting countries may supply a different product to allies than to neutral or hostile buyers. Importers may prefer to support the producers of allied countries or they may prefer to diversify their purchases among suppliers for security reasons. If a country relies heavily on imports for its supply of a good, it may want to minimize the probability of restricted supply by diversifying its purchases. The latter is characteristic of the Japanese Wheat Board import policy. This policy is a variant of the demand behavior of risk averse traders mentioned by Branson (1972).

Two additional reasons for treating commodities as nonhomogeneous are unrelated to importers' perceptions of the quality or variety of a good. The third refers to the time aggregation problem mentioned earlier. If yearly trade flows are estimated, cross-hauling is likely to occur because of variations in harvest time across countries. Even if a good is homogeneous so that importers do not differentiate their demand by supplier, over a year two-way trade is likely to occur. In that case, the trade pattern will look as if the good were heterogeneous even though it may be homogeneous in the minds of importers.

Fourth, Branson's case of monopolistic competition can be extended to include any degree of imperfect competition where suppliers' shares of the market vary. That is, a homogeneous commodity traded by a few countries may be modeled as if it were heterogeneous as long as all export shares are not equal. Given a market demand elasticity, demand elasticities facing each supplier must vary if market shares vary. To state the most obvious example, a country supplying half the world's supply of a good will face a less elastic demand than a country supplying one-tenth of the world demand.

Given any of the above conditions, a model distinguishing among products on the basis of their geographical origin is a useful abstraction. Thus, there are n separate markets for good i in such a model, n producer prices of good i, and n^2 consumer prices, where n is the number of trading countries. In general, the problem posed by such a model is that the number of parameters to be estimated is unmanageable for trade models of more than a few countries. That is, for a model of m goods, potentially there are mn^2 product own-price elasticities and $mn^2(n - 1)$ product cross price elasticities of demand. Models that distinguish goods by place of production, then, generally place restrictions on the import demand functions in order to reduce the parameter space.

IMF MODELS

The IMF models by Armington (1969a) and by Artus and Rhomberg (1973) and Rhomberg (1970) explicitly place restrictions on the form of the demand equations. Both models assume that the marginal rates of substitution between two products of one kind are independent of products of another kind. In the case of wheat, that would mean that the rate at which consumers substitute wheat produced by one country for that produced by another does not depend on their purchases of a kind of rice, for example. In a model of more than one good, that assumption reduces the number of parameters to be estimated in the following way. If there are m goods and n countries (and therefore mn products), then one country's demand for one product is a function of (m + n) price variables rather than mn where no assumptions are made concerning independence of marginal rates of substitution.

In addition to the independence assumption, Armington made the following assumptions: (2) the elasticities of substitution between products of a kind competing in a market are constant; and (3) the elasticities of substitution between any two products of a kind competing in a market equal the elasticity between any other two products of that kind competing in that market. An example in terms of wheat is the following: the percentage change in relative amounts of U.S. and Canadian wheat purchased in Germany in response to a percentage change in the price of U.S. relative to Canadian wheat is a constant; and the percentage change in the relative amounts of U.S. and Canadian wheat purchased in Germany in response to the price change equals the percentage change in relative amounts of U.S. and Argentine wheat that would be purchased in Germany in response to a change in the price of U.S. wheat relative to Argentine wheat.

These two assumptions are sufficient conditions for the percentage change in the quantity demanded of a product to be expressed as an additive function of percentage changes in expenditure on the good and percentage changes in relevant prices. That is, if prices do not change, the demand equations state that a country exporting a particular product will maintain its share of the market for that good. This is equivalent to saying that the elasticity of demand for a product (for example, U.S. wheat) with respect to expenditure on the good (wheat) is unity for all products (any country's wheat). Also the coefficients of the percentage price change variables are price elasticities of demand for the product which can be calculated from trade data and elasticities of demand for the good. That is, the n^2 demand equations for a good can be stated as

$$\dot{Q}_j^k = f(\dot{D}^k, \dot{P}_i^k, \ldots, \dot{P}_n^k)$$
$$= \dot{D}^k + \sum_{h=1}^{n} \eta_{jh}^k \dot{P}_h^k \qquad\qquad 1$$

where

$j, h, k = 1, \ldots, n$

$\dot{Q}_j^k$ = percentage change in quantity demanded (volume) in country k of country j's product,

$\dot{D}^k$ = percentage change in country k's expenditure on the good,

$\dot{P}_j^k$ = percentage change in the price of country j's product in country k, and

η_{jh}^k = country k's price elasticity of demand for the good produced by country j with respect to the price of the good produced by country h.

There are n possible supply equations for the good:

$$\dot{q}_j = f(p_j, W_j)$$

2

$$= a_j \dot{p}_j + W_j$$

where

$\dot{q}_j$ = percentage in quantity supplied of country j's product in terms of volume,

W_j = exogenous supply shifter in country j,

a_j = supply elasticity for country j's product,

$\dot{p}_j$ = percentage change in the producer price for j's product.

The coefficients of the price variable are the supply elasticities (in volume terms). In the case of wheat, these usually would be acreage estimates, so the exogenous supply shifter is included so that the quantity supplied reflects weather changes or any other exogenous shock affecting supply (production subsidies, quotas).

The prices in the demand and supply equations are linked by n^2 identities:

$$\dot{P}_j^k = \dot{p}_j + L_j^k$$

3

where L_j^k = exogenous shifter. It is through L_j^k that changes in transport costs, exchange rates, or trade barriers can be introduced.

As long as $\dot{D}^k$ is exogenous, the model is completed by n equilibrium conditions:

$$\dot{q}_j = \sum_{k=1}^{n} \frac{\dot{Q}_j^k}{Q_j} \dot{Q}_j^k$$

4

where

$$\dot{q}_j = \sum_{k=1}^{n} q_j^k .$$

It is assumed that each market clears initially so that any change in demand must be offset by a change in supply.

The model of Artus and Rhomberg is slightly different. They do assume (1), but instead of (2) and (3) they assume the following: (4) the ratios of elasticities of substitution between products are constant; and (5) the elasticity of substitution between two products of a kind in import markets is equal for all import markets while the elasticity of substitution between two products can be different abroad and in the home market. As in the case of Armington's model, these assumptions greatly reduce the number of parameters to be estimated and allow the included parameter coefficients to be easily calculated.

These types of models have several advantages over spatial equilibrium models. First, if for some reason consumers prefer one type of wheat to another, these models allow the trade flow pattern to be influenced by that preference. As noted earlier, such preferences would not affect trade flows in the spatial models unless constraints were added to reflect them. This advantage follows from two things: (1) the IMF-type models distinguish goods by place of production, and (2) trade flows in the IMF models are based on past trade data rather than determined by optimization of some objective function. Second, they do not restrict the numbers of multilateral trade flows in the trade matrix, whereas the spatial models do.

The Armington-type models are not without critics (Houthakker 1972; Branson 1972). However, most of the criticism is concerned with the theoretical underpinnings of his particular model, especially the kind of utility function he imposes. Additionally, the use of the Armington-type models for Standard International Trade Classifications (SITC) of more than one digit generally has been considered implausible (Labys 1973 and 1975; Taplin 1967). That is, commodity groupings such as wheat, feed grains, or rice have been considered homogeneous. As we pointed out earlier, however, price data and trade patterns for wheat are consistent with the view that consumers act as if they distinguish among alternative suppliers. Since the validity of any model is in its ability to predict, there is no reason, a priori, to reject this type of model.

TRUMAN-RESNICK APPROACH

Truman and Resnick (1973, 1974) have developed a similar technique for determining international trade flows, and they have applied it to the aggregate trade of the EEC and European Free Trade Association (EFTA) countries. They determined total nonagricultural imports for each country and their distribution among suppliers. The main objective of the study was to investigate the effect of alternative tariff structures on West European trade flows.

A direct application of the Truman-Resnick model to wheat would yield a matrix of world trade flows. Prices must be determined exogenously and total wheat imports for each region are determined by the relative prices of imported and domestic wheat as well as other standard demand variables. In this first stage, imports from different sources are treated as perfect substitutes for each other but imperfect substitutes for domestic wheat. These restrictions are the same as those imposed by Artus and Rhomberg. That is, U.S. and Canadian wheat are imperfect substitutes in their own national markets but perfect substitutes in all other world markets.

After determining total imports for each region, a second stage distributes imports among suppliers based on relative prices. Thus, French consumers, who previously were indifferent between U.S. and Canadian wheat, will now discriminate between them in determining import shares. This procedure determines a world trade matrix in wheat based on current prices and parameters estimated from historical trade data. No direct use of transport cost data is made, since they are already incorporated into import prices. In this respect the Truman-Resnick approach is like Armington's model and unlike spatial models.

The major shortcoming of the Truman-Resnick approach from our perspective is that prices are not determined by the model. Prices could be incorporated by introducing supply equations, but this approach seems more cumbersome than working directly with the Armington model.

REFERENCES

Adams, F. Gerard and Jere R. Behrman. 1976. *Econometric Models of World Agricultural Commodity Markets*. Cambridge, Mass.: Ballinger.

Armington, Paul S. 1969a. "A Theory of Demand for Products Distinguished by Place of Production." *International Monetary Fund Staff Papers* 16 (March): 159-78.

——. 1969b. "The Geographic Pattern of Trade and the Effects of Trade and the Effects of Price Changes." *International Monetary Fund Staff Papers* 16 (July): 179-99.

——. 1970a. "A Many-Country Model of Equilibrating Adjustments in Prices and Spending." *International Monetary Fund Staff Papers* 17 (March): 23-26.

——. 1970b. "Adjustment of Trade Balances: Some Experiments with a Model of Trade Among Many Countries." *International Monetary Fund Staff Papers* 17 (November): 488-517.

——. 1973. "A Note on Income-Compensated Price Elasticities of Demand Used in the Multilateral Exchange Rate Model." *International Monetary Fund Staff Papers* 20 (November): 608-11.

Artus, Jacques and Rudolf Rhomberg. 1973. "A Multilateral Exchange Rate Model," *International Monetary Fund Staff Papers* 20 (November): 591-608.

Ball, R. J., ed. 1973. *The International Linkage of National Economic Models*. Amsterdam: North-Holland.

Bawden, D. Lee. 1966. "A Spatial Price Equilibrium Model of International Trade." *Journal of Farm Economics* 48 (November): 862-74.

Bjarnason, Harold F. 1967. "An Economic Analysis of 1980 International Trade in Feed Grains." Ph.D. dissertation, Department of Economics, University of Wisconsin, Madison.

Blakeslee, Leroy, Earl Heady, and Charles Framingham. 1973. *World Food Production, Demand, and Trade*. Ames: Iowa State Press.

Branson, William H. 1972. "The Trade Effects of the 1971 Currency Realignments." *Brookings Papers on Economic Activity* (1): 15–67.

Dean, Gerald and Norman Collins. 1966. "Trade and Welfare Effects of EEC Tariff Policy: A Case Study of Oranges." *Journal of Farm Economics* 48 (November): 826–46.

Forrester, Jay W. 1971. *World Dynamics*. Cambridge, Mass.: Wright-Allen Press.

Houthakker, Hendrik. 1972. "Discussion." *Brookings Papers on Economic Activity* 1: 65–66.

Hutchinson, John, James Naive, and Sheldon Tsu. 1970. *World Demand Prospects for Wheat in 1980*. Foreign Agricultural Report 62. Washington, D.C.: U.S. Department of Agriculture.

Johnson, Paul R. 1971. *Studies in the Demand for U.S. Exports of Agricultural Commodities*. Economics Research Report No. 15. Raleigh: North Carolina State University.

Judge, George G. and Takashi Takayama. 1973. *Studies in Economic Planning Over Space and Time*. Amsterdam: North-Holland.

Kennedy, Michael. 1974. "An Economic Model of the World Oil Market." *Bell Journal of Economics and Management Science* 5 (Autumn): 540–77.

Kost, William E. 1975. "Trade Flows in the Grain-Livestock Economy of the European Economic Community." in *Quantitative Models of Commodity Markets*, ed. Walter C. Labys, Cambridge, Mass.: Ballinger.

Labys, Walter C. 1973. *Dynamic Commodity Models: Specification, Estimation, and Simulation*. Lexington, Mass.: Heath.

——, ed. 1975. *Quantitative Models of Commodity Markets*. Cambridge, Mass.: Ballinger.

Meadows, Donella H. et al. 1972. *The Limits to Growth*. New York: Universe Books.

Nordhaus, William D. 1973. "World Dynamics: Measurement Without Data," *Economic Journal* 83 (December): 1156–83.

Rhomberg, Rudolf. 1970. "Possible Approaches to a Model of World Trade and Payments." *International Monetary Fund Staff Papers* 17 (March): 1–22.

Rojko, Anthony, Francis Urban and James Naive. 1971. *World Demand Prospects for Grain in 1980*. Foreign Agricultural Economic Report 75. Washington, D.C.: U.S. Department of Agriculture.

Samuelson, Paul. 1952. "Spatial Price Equilibrium and Linear Programming." *American Economic Review* 42 (June): 283–303.

Schmitz, Andrew. 1968. "An Economic Analysis of the World Wheat Economy in 1980." Ph.D. dissertation, Department of Agricultural Economics, University of Wisconsin, Madison.

Schmitz, Andrew and D. Lee Bawden. 1973. *The World Wheat Economy: An Empirical Analysis*. Giannini Foundation Monograph no. 32, Berkeley, Calif.

Solow, Robert. 1972. "Notes on 'Doomsday Models.'" *Proceedings of the National Academy of Sciences* 69, no. 12.

Taplin, Grant. 1967. "Models of World Trade." *International Monetary Fund Staff Papers* 14 (November): 433-55.

Truman, Edwin M. and Stephen A. Resnick. 1973. "An Empirical Examination of Bilateral Trade in Western Europe." *Journal of International Economics* 3 (November): 305-35.

Truman, Edwin M. 1974. "The Distribution of West European Trade Under Alternative Tariff Policies." *Review of Economics and Statistics* 56 (February): 83-91.

United Nations. 1974. *World Grain Trade Statistics 1973-74*. Rome: Food and Agriculture Organization.

U.S. Department of Agriculture. 1974. *Wheat Situation*. Washington, D.C.: U.S. Government Printing Office.

Wallace, T. D. 1963. "The General Problem of Spatial Equilibrium: A Methodological Issue." In King, Richard, ed. *Interregional Competition*. Raleigh: Agricultural Policy Institute, North Carolina State University.

4

WORLD
WHEAT TRADE
MODEL

For our problem we have followed the approach of the IMF models by Armington in which consumers discriminate among products on the basis of their geographical origin. The world is decomposed into six endogenous regions and an exogenous rest of the world (ROW). The six include the four major exporters (United States, Canada, Australia, and Argentina) and two major importers (Japan, EEC). Supply is taken as exogenous, so the main output of the model is to predict the effects on prices and world trade flows of given changes in supply and other outside variables.

The three basic assumptions underlying the model are:

1. The marginal rate of substitution between any two kinds of wheat is independent of any other goods in the consumer's market basket.

2. The elasticity of substitution between any two kinds of wheat in a given market is a constant.

3. The elasticity of substitution between any two kinds of wheat in a given market equals the elasticity of substitution between any other kinds of the good in the same market.

DEMAND

The demand for any particular wheat flow can be stated as:*

$$DIJ = EXIJ + \eta_{ijj} DPIJ + \sum_{\substack{h \neq j}}^{5} \eta_{ijh} + \sum_{k=1}^{m} \eta_{ijk} DPIK \qquad 1$$

where

m = number of other goods,

DIJ = percentage change in quantity of country J's wheat going to country I,

EXIJ = percentage change in country I's expenditure on country J's wheat expressed in terms of country J's currency,

DPIJ = percentage change in the price of country J's wheat in country I, expressed in terms of country J's currency,

DPIK = percentage change in the price of good k in country I,

η_{ijh} = price elasticity of demand for country J's wheat in country I with respect to the price of country H's wheat, and

η_{ijk} = price elasticity of demand for country J's wheat in country I with respect to the price of good k in country I.

EXIJ is exogenous and is equal to the percentage change in the country's income multiplied by its income elasticity of demand for all wheat (see Appendix to this chapter). The coefficient of EXIJ is unity because of the assumptions made concerning the substitutability of products. That is, assumptions 2 and 3 above imply that each country's elasticity of demand for the wheat produced by a particular country with respect to expenditure on wheat is unity. This means that an increase in income (ceteris paribus) in any country will lead to equal increases in its expenditures on all kinds of wheat. It should be noted, however, that assumptions 2 and 3 place no restrictions on the value of a country's income elasticity of demand for all wheat.

---

*Derivation of equation 1 is given in the Appendix to this chapter. Since these are the form of Armington's demand functions, that Appendix follows closely his work (1969a). Note that the variables in these demand equations are in terms of percentage changes. As shown in the Appendix, they could just as easily be stated in terms of levels with the same parameters (elasticities). Levels can easily be recaptured from knowledge of changes, and there are some computation and interpretive advantages to formulating the equations as changes.

Since we specify six endogenous countries (regions), there are potentially 36 trade flows, therefore 36 demand equations. The potential flows between the endogenous countries and the rest of the world are shown in Table 4.1. If all flows exist, then there would be 36 direct elasticities of the form η_{ijj} where the country of the last subscript is the same as the second; that is, the price of concern is the same as the wheat being supplied. In addition, there would be 180 cross elasticities for various kinds of wheat.

The Armington-type restrictions greatly reduce the number of parameters as well as the number of estimates necessary to derive them. Assumptions 1–3 allow us to generate all the necessary parameters from 12 basic parameters. The required parameters are a basic price elasticity for all wheat (in our case) in each region and an elasticity of substitution for each region. The individual demand elasticities are then found as follows:

$$\eta_{ijj} = (-1) \left[(1 - S_{ij})\sigma_i + S_{ij}(\eta_i) \right] \qquad\qquad 2$$

and

$$\eta_{ijh} = S_{ih}(\sigma_i - \eta_i) \qquad\qquad 3$$

TABLE 4.1

Wheat Demand

	Consumer						
Producer	United States	Canada	Argentina	Australia	Europe	Japan	Rest of the World
United States	DUU	DCU*	DGU	DAU	DEU	DJU	DRU
Canada	DUC*	DCC	DGC*	DAC*	DEC	DJC	DRC
Argentina	DUG*	DCG*	DGG	DAG*	DEG	DJG*	DRG
Australia	DUA*	DCA*	DGA*	DAA	DEA	DJA	DRA
Europe	DUE*	DCE*	DGE*	DAE*	DEE	DJE*	DRE
Japan	DUJ*	DCJ*	DGJ*	DAJ*	DEJ*	DJJ	DRJ
Rest of the World	DUR	DCR	DGR	DAR	DER	DJR	DRR

Notes: DIJ = percentage change in the demand of country I for country J's wheat.
Rest of the World = exogenous regions.
*Indicates the potential flow is in fact zero or negligible.
Source: Compiled by the authors.

where the η_{ijj} and η_{ijh} are as defined and σ_i is the elasticity of substitution in market i, η_i is the basic demand elasticity in market i, and S_{ih} is the share of H's wheat in market i, and all elasticities are given positive signs for convenience. The reader is referred to the Appendix for the derivation of η_{ijj} and η_{ijh}.

SUPPLY

A model of the kind being considered would in general include six endogenous quantity supplied variables. These variables would be functions of domestic supply prices and various exogenous supply shifters. Total supply to the market of a particular wheat (TSJ) is the sum of production (SJ) and net sales from inventories (NJ). Both of these sources are determined outside the model, so the percentage change in total supplies of each of the six regions (DTSJ's) is an exogenous variable.

PRICE EQUATIONS

The model potentially includes 36 price equations of the general form:

DPIJ = SPJ + LIJ　　　　　　　　　　　　　　　　　4

where SPJ is the percentage change in the supply price in country J (expressed in J's currency) and the LIJ are exogenous shifters.

An equation such as 4 says that the change in the consumer price in I for a flow from J is equal to the change in the producer price in J plus any change in the margin between these two prices. It is here that changes in the exchange rate between country I and J, in freight rates or other transportation costs, tariff or other tax (or subsidy) changes can be entered.

Where the exogenous variable and the supply price are related to the demand price multiplicatively, the form of DPIJ given by equation 4 is used. For example, exchange rate changes or ad valorem tariffs, such would be the case since

$$PIJ = P_j^S(T_j^i)$$

where

PIJ = demand price of J's wheat in country I (in country I's currency),

P_j^S = supply price of J's wheat (in J's currency),

T_j^i = price of J's currency in terms of I's currency.

DPIJ then would be an additive function of SPJ and dT_j^i/T_j^i.

If, however, PIJ is an additive function of the supply price and exogenous variable DPIJ becomes

$$DPIJ = \frac{P_j^s}{PIJ} dT_j^i + \frac{T_j^i}{PIJ} dP_j^s + LIJ \qquad\qquad 4'$$

where

  LIJ = KIJ/PIJ,
  PIJ = $P_j^s (T_j^i)$ + KIJ, and
  KIJ = exogenous price distortion.

Equation 4' would be the correct specification for DPIJ, for example, where the exogenous shifter is a change in transport costs.

Since it can be said that the exogenous shocks "drive" the model, the LIJ terms are crucial in predicting changes. Of course, their impact is only determined when the model is solved for the endogenous variables.

EQUILIBRIUM CONDITIONS

There are six market-clearing conditions that close the model. Since the model is specified in percentage changes in variables, these equations state that the percentage changes in demand for a particular country must equal the percentage changes in quantity supplied by that country. Thus:

$$DTSJ = \sum_{I=1}^{n} (\frac{IJ}{J})DIJ \qquad\qquad 5$$

where $(\frac{IJ}{J})$ is the proportion of J's wheat that does to country I. If these proportions stay the same through time, this model belongs to the class of models that have become known as constant market share models.

Since our model consists of six endogenous regions, it potentially consists of n^2 = 36 demand equations, n^2 = 36 price equations, and n = 6 market-clearing equations. However, empirical considerations simplify the model, since 23 of the 36 potential trade flows are zero or negligible. This reduces the number of endogenous variables from 36 + 36 + 6 = 78 to 13 + 13 + 6 = 32.

GOVERNMENT POLICY IN THE TRADE MODEL

Government policy is introduced into the model through the set of price equations that relate the supply price of wheat in each exporting country to the corresponding prices of the same wheat in the importing countries. These equations take the following general form of equation 4,* that is,

---

*As noted earlier, equation 4' is the appropriate specification of DPIJ in some cases.

DPIJ = SPJ + LIJ

where DPIJ is the percentage change in the demand price (facing millers) in importing country I, SPJ is the percentage change in the supply price in country J, and LIJ is the set of percentage changes in exogenous variables through which policy enters. These consist of transport costs, marketing margins, trade controls, and exchange rates. Recall that all of the above variables are expressed as percentage changes, so that for constant levels of the LIJs, an X percent rise in the price of wheat in the United States will result in an X percent rise in the price of U.S. wheat in Europe and Japan. Also an X percent increase in the LIJs involving the United States will cause an increase in the demand prices in Europe and Japan and a decrease in the supply price in the United States which sums to X percent.

The LIJs play an important role in the model, but their exogenous nature precludes the model from providing information about them. Thus a major task of the user of the model is to acquire information about these variables from other sources. Some variables such as tariffs and buy/sell prices of state trading agencies are announced in advance, others such as transport costs and real exchange rates may require a separate forecasting model, and others such as discretionary trade controls may require a country expert's best judgment. All of the variables must be quantified to render them comparable to other changes. This is not difficult for a change in transport costs or an export subsidy but it is more troublesome when a government discourages exports by reporting requirements and "moral suasion."

Excluding purely domestic flows, the model contains seven price equations that link exporters and importers.

U.S. exports:
DPEU = SPU + LEU
DPJU = SPU + LJU

Australian exports:
DPEA = SPI + LEA
DPJA = SPA + LJA

Canadian exports:
DPEC = SPC + LEC
DPJC = SPC + LJC

Argentine exports:
EPEG = SPG + LEG

The demand price is expressed in the currency of the importing country, but the supply price is denominated in the currency of the exporting country. All prices are real prices so the inflation rate of the exporting country must be entered as one of the LIJs. For example, an X percent revaluation of the yen (equals devaluation of the dollar) will, for a given dollar price of U.S. wheat, lower the yen price of U.S. wheat by X percent. For a given exchange rate, an X percent inflation in the United States will raise the yen price of U.S. wheat by X percent. Thus, a combination of an X percent U.S. inflation and an X percent devaluation will leave the yen price of U.S. sheat unchanged. Exchange rate changes that are purely monetary in the sense of following purchasing power parity considerations do not affect the model. Currrency changes caused by real forces (cost, demand, capital flows) do alter relative prices and the structure of trade. Notice also than an X percent U.S. export subsidy (tax) to Japan has the same effect on prices and trade as an X percent import subsidy (tariff) in Japan or an X percent reduction in transport costs between the United States and Japan. Thus, the model abstracts from the question of who receives the tariff revenue, raises the revenue for a subsidy, or receives transport revenue. Similarly in trade relations with ROW, the model does not distinguish between commercial sales or gifts.

Of the four classes of exogenous variables mentioned above, we have introduced information on all but marketing margins. They enter the model in the same way as the other three, but we have not found a convenient and reliable source of information on them. Representing the remaining variables, trade controls, transport costs, and exchange has been easier for some countries and variables than for others. Historical transport costs are readily available from the International Wheat Council, but since they are volatile, they may not be easy to determine in advance. Past inflation rates are available from the Organization for Economic Cooperation and Development (OECD) and the IMF and a number of forecasting models are accessible. Past exchange rates are available from the IMF but future rates present a problem. Organized forward markets exist for all the major currencies with the possible exception of Argentina; so one could use forward quotations for one year in advance as a proxy for future spot rates.

Trade controls are less tractable because they take many different institutional forms, and it is difficult to quantify some of them and difficult to obtain information that is both current and accurate on all of them. On the import side the important institutions are the Japan Food Agency, which is the sole importer of wheat, and the EEC's Common Agricultural Policy, which controls imports through its variable levy and currency controls. On the export side, the Canadian and Australian Wheat Boards are domestic monopolists in marketing. Although it has returned to private trading, Argentina has controlled exports through taxes, quotas, and multiple exchange rates until the past year. The United States has employed export subsidies and limited quantitative controls. Of course wheat policy in ROW is important to the model, but it is treated in the same exogenous fashion as all economic behavior in ROW.

The effective export tax or subsidy levied by the Canadian or Australian Wheat boards can be expressed as the excess of the export price over the domestic price to millers. Thus we define the export tax per unit in period t as

$$T_t = P_t^X - P_t^D \qquad\qquad 5$$

As noted earlier, DPIJ takes the form 4' when the exogenous shifter has this form. That is, the percentage change in the export tax is not entered as LIJ = $(T_t - T_{t-1})/(T_t)$. Assuming domestic price distortions to be equal to zero,* the tax is equal to the percentage change in the export price; or

$$LIJ = \frac{(P_t^D + T_t) - (P_t^D + T_{t-1})}{P_t^D + T} = \frac{T_t - T_{t-1}}{P_t^D + T_t} \qquad 6$$

where

P_t^D = domestic price to millers,

P_t^S = domestic supply price = P_t^D, and

T_t = export tax.

For example consider the following data for Canada:

	P_t^X	P_t^D	T_t
1972–73	$91.99	$91.99	0
1973–74	$201.69	$119.40	$82.29

$$LIC = \frac{(P_{73}^D + T_{73}) - (P_{73}^D + T_{72})}{P_{73}^D + T_{73}}$$

$$= \frac{(119.40 + 82.29) - (119.40 + 0)}{201.69}$$

---

*If there are any domestic price distortions driving a wedge between the domestic supply price and the domestic price to millers then equation 5 would be:

$$T_t = P_t^X - p_t^S \qquad 5'$$

Accordingly 6 would become

$$LIJ = \frac{(P_t^S + T_t) - (P_t^S + T_{t-1})}{P_t^S + T_t} = \frac{T_t - T_{t-1}}{p_t^S + T_t} \qquad 6'$$

The domestic price distortion would enter the model through DPII as

$$KII = P_t^D - P_t^S$$

so that

$$LII = \frac{(P_t^D - P_t^S) - (P_{t-1}^D - P_{t-1}^S)}{P_t^D} .$$

= +40.8 percent.

This is interpreted as a 40.8 percent increase in Canada's export tax to Japan and EEC in 1973-74.

An analogous procedure is used to calculate the effective tariff and its rate of change levied by the Japan Food Agency. Define the tariff per unit as

$$T_t = P_t^D - P_t^I$$

where P_t^I is the import price at time t. The percent change in the tariff is

$$LJI = \frac{(P_t^I + T_t) - (P_t^I + T_{t-1})}{(P_t^I + T_t)}$$

For the historical period the EEC tariff was calculated in the same manner, but since the variable levy is a function of the current import price, the levy also becomes an endogenous variable in forecasting problems. The determination of the levy and border taxes by EEC authorities is rather complicated. For details see Josling and Harris (1976).

To illustrate the role of the policy variables, consider their behavior in the 1970s. The outstanding event of the 1970s in wheat markets has been the substantial increase in wheat prices. The import price at Rotterdam averaged about $70 per ton in the decade ending 1972, but in 1974 prices rose to well over $200 per ton. The policy response of governments was rather uniform as nearly everyone attempted to force the price adjustment on to someone else. Importing countries subsidized imports and exporting countries discouraged exports. Since this reduced the number of adjusting markets, the price increases in the remaining markets were greater than would have otherwise occurred. As we show in Chapter 7, government policy that attempted to stabilize domestic wheat prices had the effect of destabilizing external prices, because world excess demand was increased by adding to import demand and subtracting from export supply. And we show in Chapter 8 that since trade and inventories can be considered substitutes, the trade policy of the 1970s made wheat inventories less adequate in stabilizing prices than they otherwise would have been, since they increased the excess demand that could have been satisfied by sales from inherited inventories.

The specific trade policies that added to world wheat shortage were the following. Prior to 1973 the Japan Food Agency imported wheat at the world price and imposed a small tariff by reselling at a higher price. However, as world prices rose, the agency insulated consumers from the price rise by selling domestically at a loss, and this effective import subsidy continued from 1973 until January 1976. The EEC sought the same kind of insulation for its consumers by adjusting its variable levy. In the five years preceding 1973, the levy exceeded $50 per ton, but as world prices rose, the levy was reduced to zero in September

1973 and remained there until January 1975. In addition, border taxes and subsidies were imposed to offset currency changes and an export tax, which eventually rose to $100 per ton in February 1974, was imposed for sales to certain regions while exports to other regions were banned. The net effect was to keep EEC wheat prices below world wheat prices, which was a major change in this relationship. In 1971-73, internal wheat prices were 209 percent of world prices, in 1972-73 they were 153 percent, and in 1973-74 they were 79 percent. The EEC pursued a similar policy of insulation with regard to corn and rice as well.

All four exporters restricted their sales, although the United States employed mild restrictions in the form of advance reporting of foreign sales. Beginning in 1973 Canada effectively taxed exports by selling to domestic millers at C$3.25 (this was announced as a seven-year program) when export prices averaged more than $5.00 per bushel. The Australian Wheat Board has pursued a similar policy of taxing wheat exports since 1973, and at times the export price was twice the domestic consumption price. Argentina embargoed wheat for part of 1973, and since lifting the embargo they have taxed wheat exports with an increasingly punitive exchange rate. Argentina has also vacillated between a state trading monopoly and private exporters. In addition to the policies of our endogenous countries, many countries in ROW such as India, China, Pakistan, and USSR attempted to insulate their economies in the 1970s by subsidizing imports.

APPENDIX: DERIVATION OF PRODUCT DEMAND FUNCTIONS

As noted in the text, country k's demand for country j's product in a one-good, n country model can be represented by equation 1 if the following conditions hold:

1. the marginal rate of substitution between any two kinds of a good is independent of any other goods in the consumer's market basket;
2. the elasticity of substitution between any two kinds of a good in a given market is a constant; and
3. the elasticity of substitution between any two kinds of a good in a given market equals the elasticity of substitution between any other kinds of a good in the same market.

These assumptions imply that an importer's purchasing decision can be represented by a two-stage budgeting procedure.* In the first stage, the importer

---

*Armington (1969a), Strotz (1957), Pearce (1971), Bieri and deJanvry (1972), Barten (1977) and Green (1964).

determines expenditure on goods by maximizing

$$U = U(Q_1, \ldots, Q_m) \tag{A.1}$$

subject to

$$E = \sum_{i=1}^{m} Q_i P_i \tag{A.2}$$

where

    U = total utility,
    E = total expenditure,
    Q_i = quantity index for good i, and
    P_i = price index for good i.

The resulting demand for each good, Q_i, is a function of m good prices and total expenditure,

$$Q_i = Q_i(P_1, \ldots, P_m, E) \tag{A.3}$$

or in terms of expenditure for each good

$$E_i = P_i Q_i(P_1, \ldots, P_m, E) \tag{A.4}$$

Product demands are determined by allocating expenditure on each good, E_i, so that Q_i is maximized. That is, the quantity index Q_i represents utility derived from consuming products of that kind, and the importer wants to maximize the utility derived from his predetermined expendiure on good i.* The utility index implied by assumptions 2 and 3 is:

$$Q_i = \phi_i(Q_{i1}, \ldots, Q_{in}) \tag{A.5}$$

$$= [\sum_{j=1}^{n} b_{ij} Q_{ij}^{-\rho_i}]^{-1/\rho_i}$$

where

---

*This is equivalent to minimizing the cost of purchasing a predetermined amount of good i. That is, Q_i is determined in stage 1 and each importer wants to allocate his purchases among suppliers so as to minimize E_i.

Q_{ij} = quantity of good i produced by country j,

$\sigma_i = 1/(1 + \rho_i)$ = elasticity of substitution of products of good i. Maximization of Q_i subject to E_i yields the $n + 1$ equations

$$b_{ij}[\frac{Q_i}{Q_{ij}}]^{1/\sigma_i} - \lambda_i P_{ij} = 0 \qquad\qquad\qquad A.6$$

$$E_i - \sum_j P_{ij} Q_{ij} = 0 \qquad\qquad\qquad A.7$$

where

P_{ij} = consumer price of good i supplied by country j, and

λ_i = Langrangian multiplier for maximization of Q_i.

These first-order conditions yield demand equations of the following form:

$$Q_{ij} = f_i(P_{i1}, \ldots, P_{in}, E_i)$$
$$= E_i[\frac{P_{ij}}{b_{ij}}]^{-\sigma_i}[\sum_k b_{ik}^{\sigma_i} P_{ik}^{1-\sigma_i}]^{-1} \quad \text{for } j = 1, \ldots, n \qquad A.8$$

$$\lambda_i = f_i(P_{i1}, \ldots, P_{in}, E_i)$$
$$= E_i^{-1/\sigma_i}[\sum_j b_{ij}^{-\sigma_i} P_{ij}^{1-\sigma_i} Q_i]^{1/\sigma_i} \qquad\qquad A.9$$

Because ϕ_i given by A.5 is linearly homogeneous (Solow 1955–56), the n first order conditions given by A.8 can also be expressed as

$$P_i = P_{ij} b_{ij}^{-1}[\frac{Q_{ij}}{Q_i}]^{1/\sigma_i} \qquad\qquad\qquad A.10$$

Substituting A.10 into A.8 simplifies the n demands for Q_{ij} to*

$$Q_{ij} = b_{ij}^{\sigma_i} Q_i[\frac{P_{ij}}{P_i}]^{-\sigma_i} \qquad\qquad\qquad A.11$$

---

*Since the original application of this demand structure to world trade models was in forecasting balance-of-payments effects of policies (Armington assumptions 1–3), the demand functions are often stated in value terms or

$$P_{ij} Q_{ij} = b_{ij}^{\sigma_i} P_i X_i[\frac{P_{ij}}{P_i}]^{1-\sigma_i} \qquad\qquad\qquad A.11'$$

Percentage Changes in Product Demand

The percentage change in Q_{ij} can be derived by totally differentiating A.11 and A.3, then substituting the differential of A.3 into the differential of A.11. The differential of A.11 divided by Q_{ij} is

$$\frac{dQ_{ij}}{Q_{ij}} = \frac{dQ_i}{Q_i} - \sigma_i \left[\frac{dP_{ij}}{P_{ij}} - \frac{dP_i}{P_i}\right]. \qquad \text{A.12}$$

The differential of A.3 divided by Q_i is

$$\frac{dQ_i}{Q_i} = \epsilon_i \frac{dE}{E} - \eta_{i/i} \frac{dP_i}{P_i} + \sum_{g \neq i} \eta_{i/g} \frac{dP_g}{P_g} \qquad \text{A.13}$$

A.13 substituted into A.12 is

$$\frac{dQ_{ij}}{Q_{ij}} = \epsilon_i \frac{dE}{E} - \eta_{i/i} \frac{dP_i}{P_i} + \sum_{g \neq i} \eta_{i/g} \frac{dP_g}{P_g} - \sigma_i \left[\frac{dP_{ij}}{P_{ij}} - \frac{dP_i}{P_i}\right] \qquad \text{A.14}$$

where

ϵ_i = the expenditure elasticity of demand for good i, and

$\eta_{i/g}$ = price elasticity of demand for good i with respect to the price of good g.

From A.10 it follows that the percentage change in the price of good i can be expressed as

$$\frac{dP_i}{P_i} = \sum_j S_{ij} \frac{dP_{ij}}{P_{ij}}$$

$$S_{ij} = \frac{P_{ij} Q_{ij}}{P_i Q_i} \qquad \text{A.15}$$

where $S_{ij} = P_{ij} Q_{ij}/P_i Q_i$.

A.14 can be rewritten, then,* as

---

*As mentioned above, Armington derived his percentage change equations in value terms. A.16 expressed in value terms differs only in the coefficient of dP_{ij}/P_{ij}. That is,

$$\frac{dQ_{ij}}{Q_{ij}} = \epsilon_i \frac{dE}{E} - [(1-S_{ij})\sigma_i + S_{ij}\eta_{i/i}] \frac{dP_{ij}}{P_{ij}}$$

A.16

$$+ \sum_{h \neq j} [S_{ih}\sigma_i - S_{ih}\eta_{i/i}] \frac{dP_{ih}}{P_{ih}} + \sum_{g \neq i} \eta_{i/g} \frac{dP_g}{P_g}$$

The coefficient of the first term in A. 16 is the elasticity of demand for Q_{ij} with respect to expenditure. It equals the expenditure elasticity for good i because the expenditure elasticity of Q_{ij} is unity with respect to expenditure on Q_i. This follows from the linear homogeneity of ϕ_i and can be shown by multiplying the partial derivative of A.8 with respect to E_i by (E_i/Q_{ij}).

$$\left(\frac{\partial Q_{ij}}{\partial E_i}\right) \left(\frac{E_i}{Q_{ij}}\right) = b_{ij}^{\sigma_i} P_{ij}^{-\sigma_i} P_i^{\sigma_i - 1} E_i/Q_{ij} = 1$$

A.17

The coefficients of the second and third terms on A. 16 are, respectively, the direct price elasticity of demand for Q_{ij}, and the cross-price elasticity of demand for Q_{ij}, with respect to a change in the price of another product of the same kind, P_{ih}. These elasticities correspond to Cournot price elasticities showing the combined effect of substitution among products of the same kind caused by the price change and the effect caused by the price-induced change in the good price index and, thus, in the expenditure on good i. The substitution portion of each elasticity (that is, the Slutsky elasticity) is the share-weighted elasticity of substitution and the expenditure effect is the share-weighted price elasticity of demand for the good. This can be shown by expressing the partial derivatives of A.11 with respect to P_{ij} and P_{ih} in elasticity form. In the case of P_{ij} this yields

$$\frac{\partial Q_{ij} P_{ij}}{\partial P_{ij} Q_{ij}} \bigg|_{\bar{Q}_i} = \frac{\partial Q_{ij}}{\partial P_{ij}} \frac{P_{ij}}{Q_{ij}} + \frac{\partial Q_{ij}}{\partial P_i} \frac{\partial P_i}{\partial P_{ij}} \frac{P_{ij}}{Q_{ij}}$$

$$= -\sigma_i + (\sigma_i Q_{ij} P_i^{-1}) \left[\frac{Q_{ij}}{Q_i}\right] \left[\frac{P_{ij}}{Q_{ij}}\right]$$

A.18

$$= -\sigma_i + \sigma_i S_{ij}$$

$$= (1 - S_{ij})\sigma_i.$$

$$\frac{dP_{ij}X_{ij}}{P_{ij}X_{ij}} = \epsilon_i \frac{dE}{E} - [(1-S_{ij})(\sigma_i - 1) + S_{ij}(\eta_{i/i} - 1)] \frac{dP_{ij}}{P_{ij}}$$

$$+ \sum_{h \neq j} [S_{ih}\sigma_i - S_{ih}\eta_{i/i}] \frac{dP_{ih}}{P_{ih}} + \sum_{g \neq i} \eta_{i/g} \frac{dP_g}{P_g}.$$

For the cross-price Slutsky elasticity, we find

$$\frac{\partial Q_{ij}}{\partial P_{ih}} \frac{P_{ih}}{Q_{ij}}\bigg|_{\bar{Q}_i} = \frac{\partial Q_{ij}}{\partial P_{ih}} \frac{P_{ih}}{Q_{ij}} + \frac{\partial Q_{ij}}{\partial P_i} \frac{\partial P_i}{\partial P_{ih}} \frac{P_{ih}}{Q_{ij}}$$

$$= (\sigma_i Q_{ij} P_i^{-1}) \left[\frac{Q_{ih}}{Q_i}\right] \left[\frac{P_{ih}}{Q_{ij}}\right] \qquad\qquad\text{A.19}$$

$$= \sigma_i S_{ih}$$

In the case of this cross-price substitution term the only substitutability is the result of the general competition of products of kind i for the importer's income. Since the specific cross-substitution term is zero, the Slutsky cross-price elasticities depend on the share of the product whose price is changing rather than the share of the product demanded. All cross-price elasticities with respect to P_{ih} are therefore equal.

These properties can also be shown in terms of Frisch's money flexibility, ω:

$$\omega_i = (\partial \lambda_i/\partial E_i)(E_i/\lambda_i) \qquad\qquad\text{A.20}$$

Because ϕ_i is linearly homogeneous, ω is a constant. This is shown by expressing the partial elasticity of A.9 with respect to E_i in elasticity form:

$$\omega_i = -\frac{1}{\sigma_i} E_i^{\left(\frac{-1-\sigma_i}{\sigma_i}\right)} \left[\sum_j b_{ij}^{-\sigma_i} P_{ij}^{1-\sigma_i} Q_i\right]^{1/\sigma_i} E^{(\sigma_i+1)\sigma_i}$$

$$\left[\sum_j b_{ij}^{-\sigma_i} P_{ij}^{1-\sigma_i} Q_i\right]^{-1/\sigma_i} \qquad\qquad\text{A.21}$$

$$= -\frac{1}{\sigma_i}$$

The Slutsky elasticity can be expressed as

$$\frac{\partial Q_{ij}}{\partial P_{ih}} \frac{P_{ih}}{Q_{ij}}\bigg|_{\bar{Q}_i} = -\frac{\lambda_i}{\partial \lambda_i/\partial E_i} \frac{\partial Q_{ij}}{\partial E_i} \frac{\partial Q_{ih}}{\partial E_i} \frac{P_{ih}}{Q_{ij}}$$

$$= -\sigma_i E_i \left[\frac{Q_{ij}}{E_i}\right] \left[\frac{Q_{ih}}{E_i}\right] \left[\frac{P_{ih}}{Q_{ij}}\right]$$

$$= -\sigma_i \frac{Q_{ih} P_{ih}}{E_i} \qquad\qquad\text{A.22}$$

$$= -\sigma_i S_{ih}$$

REFERENCES

Armington, Paul S. 1969a. "A Theory of Demand for Products Distinguished by Place of Production." *International Monetary Fund Staff Papers* 16 (March): 159-78.

Ball, R. J., ed. 1973. *The International Linkage of National Economic Models*. Amsterdam: North-Holland.

Barten, Anton P. 1977. "The Systems of Consumer Demand Functions Approach: A Review." *Econometrica* (45): 23-51.

Bieri, Jurg, and Alain deJanvry. 1972. *Empirical Analysis of Demand Under Consumer Budgeting*. Giannini Foundation Monograph 30. Berkeley: University of California.

Branson, William H. 1972. "The Trade Effects of the 1971 Currency Realignments." *Brookings Papers on Economic Activity* (1): 15-67.

Brown, Alan, and Angus Deaton. 1972. "Models of Consumer Behavior: A Survey." *The Economic Journal* (82): 1145-1236.

Green, H. A. J. 1964. *Aggregation in Economic Analysis*. Princeton, N.J.: Princeton University Press.

International Wheat Council. *Review of the World Wheat Situation*. London.

International Wheat Council. *World Wheat Statistics*. London.

Irving, R. W., and H. A. Fearn. 1975. *Green Money and the Common Agricultural Policy*. Ashford, Kent: Centre for European Agricultural Studies.

Josling, Tim, and Simon Harris. 1976. "Europe's Green Money." *The Three Banks Review*, March, pp. 57-72.

Pearce, I. F. 1961. "An Exact Method of Consumer Demand Analysis." *Econometrica* (24): 499-516.

Strotz, Robert H. 1957. "The Empirical Implications of a Utility Tree." *Econometrica* 25 (April): 269-80.

5

APPLICATIONS
OF THE WORLD
WHEAT TRADE MODEL

Recall from Chapter 4 that the Armington-type restrictions reduce the number of parameters needed in a good model to 2n, where n is the number of countries. These basic parameters are an overall elasticity of demand in each country for the product and an elasticity of substitution for each country. Since we have adopted a common elasticity of substitution, the number of parameters is further reduced to n + 1.*

BASIC ELASTICITIES

The common elasticity of substitution used for all markets was –3.0. The basic demand elasticities used for wheat in each country are as follows:

United States	–.20	Argentina	–.30
Canada	–.20	Europe	–.30
Australia	–.10	Japan	–.33

These are judgmental values based on our own work, the work of Rojko and others in USDA, and other sources. Forecasts from the model are not as sen-

---

*All empirical implementations of this kind of model we are familiar with have also used a single elasticity of substitution for all markets. In some fairly extensive statistical testing for the Japanese and U.K. markets we were not able to reject a common elasticity value of –3.0 by conventional t tests.

sitive to small changes in these parameters as they are to shifters and policy changes. Unless the above values are completely out of line, then, these parameter estimates appear satisfactory.

Utilizing equations 2 and 3 of Chapter 4, these basic parameters can be used to generate all of the demand elasticities used. These equations are

$$\eta_{ijj} = [(-1)(1-S_{ij})\sigma_i + S_{ij}\eta_i] \qquad\qquad 2$$

$$\eta_{ijh} = S_{ij}\sigma_i - \eta_i \qquad\qquad 3$$

where σ_i and η_i are the basic elasticity and demand parameters, and s_j^i is the share of j's wheat in market i (an import share elasticity), and σ and η are defined as positive for convenience. Equation 2 yields the direct elasticities for country j's price with respect to its own wheat in market i, and equation 3 yields the cross elasticities. If all flows existed these equations would generate n^2 direct and n^2 cross elasticities. Since we do not allow all flows to enter we have used these equations to generate the elasticities shown in Tables 5.1 and 5.2.

Import shares typically change less than export shares. That is, the percentage of Japan's consumption that comes from the United States shows less change than the percentage of U.S. exports to go to Japan. Consequently these elasticities represent those based on an average of 1960s behavior and have been used throughout the study.

We performed some sensitivity analyses for varying values of basic parameters and shares. Fairly extreme changes in magnitude, approximately 100 percent of shares or basic elasticities, are required to change the calculated parameters by 10 percent, on the average. Any forecasting problems, then, do not seem to be due to the elasticity estimates.

Cross elasticities between wheat and feed grains that appear in conjunction with exogenous shifters in the model come from Rojko et al. in USDA also. The assumed values are

United States	−.10	Argentina	.05
Canada	.15	Europe	.10
Australia	0	Japan	0

SOME EXAMPLES

Our main applications of the model presented in Chapter 4 have been of a short-run forecasting nature. The other empirical applications of such models have been of a long-run equilibrium nature. The major alternative to the differentiated good model for agricultural products—the spatial equilibrium model-has also been used mainly to solve long-run equilibrium forecasts. There is no reason in principle that our model cannot be recast in longer-run terms. By the same

TABLE 5.1
Direct Price Elasticities of Demand

Consumer	United States	Canada	Australia	Argentina	Europe	Japan
			Price Change			
United States	-.228	-2.982	—	—	—	—
Canada	—	-.200	—	—	—	—
Australia	—	—	—	—	—	—
Argentina	—	—	—	-.300	—	—
Europe	-2.873	-2.870	-2.992	-2.954	-.643	—
Japan	-2.060	-2.226	-2.824	—	—	-2.223

Source: Compiled by the authors.

TABLE 5.2
Cross Price Elasticities of Demand

Consumer	United States	Canada	Australia	Argentina	Europe	Japan
			Price Change			
United States	2.772	.028	0	0	0	0
Canada	0	2.800	0	0	0	0
Australia	0	0	2.900	0	0	0
Argentina	0	0	0	2.700	0	0
Europe	.127	.130	.008	.046	2.357	0
Japan	.940	.771	.176	0	0	.777

Source: Compiled by the authors.

token there is no reason that a spatial equilibrium model cannot be interpreted in a short-run forecast sense.

As a reference point we have formulated a small spatial equilibrium model for the same endogenous countries as we use later in our model. Two sets of flow forecasts from this model are shown in Table 5.3 for the 1973–74 crop year. The flows are arranged in a trade matrix. The first set of flows is those predicted to result from the basic transport cost information with no government interference from Canada, Australia, or Japan. The basic demand parameters are the same as we use for our model. The second set of forecasts is for the same year, but now the policy restrictions discussed at length later by various countries are imposed on the solution.*

TABLE 5.3

1973–74 Trade Flow Predictions from Spatial Equilibrium Model (thousand metric tons)

From	To						
	United States	Canada	Australia	Argentina	EEC	Japan	ROW
Set 1: No government interference by Japan, Canada, and Australia							
United States	25,020	x*	x	x	0	0	26,581
Canada	x	5,162	x	x	5,169	5,212	363
Australia	x	x	2,732	x	0	0	7,965
Argentina	x	x	x	4,465	0	0	1,159
EEC	x	x	x	x	40,000	x	x
Japan	x	x	x	x	x	262	x
ROW	x	x	x	x	x	x	217,406
Set 2: Actual government policies of Japan, Canada, and Australia incorporated							
United States	24,981	x	x	x	622	0	25,998
Canada	x	5,416	x	x	4,296	6,195	0
Australia	x	x	2,844	x	0	0	7,853
Argentina	x	x	x	4,453	0	0	1,171
EEC	x	x	x	x	40,000	x	x
Japan	x	x	x	x	x	262	x
ROW	x	x	x	x	x	x	217,406

*x means trade flow not allowed.
Source: Compiled by the authors.

---

*The solutions are straightforward runs of a readily available spatial equilibrium computer software package.

TABLE 5.4

Forecast of Endogenous Variables from Exogenous
Changes in Supply
(percentage change)

	Increase U.S. Supply 10 Percent	Increase Canada 10 Percent	Increase Canada 10 Percent
DUU	7.3	1.6	4.0
DEU	80.6	−1.1	−2.75
DJU	41.5	−8.9	−22.25
DCC	2.3	5.1	12.75
DEC	13.7	5.3	13.25
DJC	−30.0	4.5	11.25
DAA	1.4	.9	2.25
DEA	22.1	2.3	5.75
DJA	−22.1	−5.5	−13.75
DGG	.9	1.0	2.5
DEG	−12.4	−13.8	−34.5
DEE	—	—	—
DJJ	0	0	0
DPUU	−35.7	−7.5	−18.75
DPEU	−35.7	−7.5	−18.75
DPJU	−35.7	−7.5	−18.75
DPCC	−11.7	−25.6	−64.0
DPEC	−11.7	−25.6	−64.0
DPJC	−11.7	−25.6	−64.0
DPAA	−14.5	−8.7	−21.75
DPEA	−14.5	−8.7	−21.75
DPJA	−14.5	−8.7	−21.75
DPGG	3.0	−3.3	−8.25
DPEG	−3.0	−3.3	−8.25
DPEE	−7.1	−7.9	−19.75
DPJJ	−21.8	−10.5	−26.25
SPU	−35.7	−7.5	−18.75
SPC	−11.7	−25.6	−64.0
SPA	−14.5	−8.7	−21.75
SPG	−3.0	−3.3	−8.25
SPE	−7.1	−7.9	−19.75
SPJ	−21.8	−10.5	−26.25

Source: Compiled by the authors.

From both sets of forecasts one can see the large degree of export specialization that is predicted from this model. The United States does not ship to
Japan in either set, they ship only a nominal amount to the EEC in the second
set. Australia and Argentina are forecast to ship only to the rest of the world. We
know that these blocked-out flows did in fact exist. Their size and our alternative forecasts are shown in Table 5.10. A direct comparison of the two models is
not really warranted at this point. The main point is the degree of specialization
implied by the spatial equilibrium model that is at variance with known market
behavior. Before turning to some actual forecasts from our model, it might prove
useful to work through some specific changes, holding other things constant to
see the internal working of the model.

Analysis of a Supply Side Change

Table 5.4 has three columns that represent forecasts of each endogenous
variable for three particular supply changes taken by themselves.* Thus the first
column shows the effect on each of the endogenous variables of a 10 percent
change in the U.S. supply of wheat and no other change taking place. Mechanic-
ally, this column is gotten by setting all entries in the exogenous shift vector to
zero except the entry in row 27 (SPU). The matrix of coefficients for these
exercises is the one that uses 1972-73 export shares. The inverse of that matrix
is then used for the solution vector of the first column by multiplying the 10
percent entry in row 27 of the shifters times the corresponding entry in each
row for column 27.

The forecast change in U.S. consumption of its own wheat, row 1 in column
1, is 7.3. This is the product of the element in column 27 of row 1 of the inverse, .73361 times 10, the exogenous change in U.S. supply. The next entry,
the forecast change in the United States to Europe flow, 80.6, is the product of
the entry in column 27, row 2, of the inverse 8.06038 times 10. These calculations are repeated for each entry in the column. As can be seen, the impact of a
10 percent U.S. supply increase, with no other exogenous shifts, would be substantial. The U.S. own flows and prices would be affected the most, but the forecast change would lower all prices considerably, from 35.7 percent in the United
States to 3.0 percent in Argentina.

The second column of changes poses a similar question of the impact on
all variables of a change in the Canadian supply, alone, of 10 percent. Again, the

---

*Throughout the symbols DIJ represents the change in the flow from country J to
country I; DPIJ represents the change in the demand price for the IJ flow; SPI represents
the change in the supply price of I. U, C, A, G, and J are the United States, Canada, Australia, Argentina, Europe, and Japan respectively.

predicted changes are large, but not as large as for the U.S. change. The last column yields predictions for a 25 percent increase in Canadian supply, which is closer in absolute amount to a 10 percent U.S. change than is a 10 percent Canadian change. All changes are predicted to go in the same direction, but the magnitudes are enlarged.

Analysis of a Price Variable Change

Table 5.5 is designed to illustrate the effect of a transport cost change on the predicted endogenous variables. The table has seven columns of forecasts for the seven export flows. Each column represents the effect on that particular flow of a 10 percent change in transport cost for that flow alone. Thus the first column shows the effect on all variables from a transport cost increase in the United States to Europe flow alone. The next six columns are calculated the same way. The last column, headed total, shows the predicted changes if transport costs went up 10 percent for all flows. The predictions are straightforward. The own flows of the major exporters increase, while all export flows (except Canada to Japan) fall. The own prices of the exporters, except Europe, fall, while the prices of the export flows rise, as do the own prices of Europe and Japan. These transport costs changes are used later in Chapter 7 to show the effect of U.S. cargo preference laws.

Analysis of a Change in Exogenous Exports

Table 5.6 illustrates the results of changing exports to the rest of the world in isolation from other changes. Column 1 shows predicted results on the endogenous variables if the United States increased their ROW exports by 10 percent and nothing else happened. Column 2 shows the forecasts if Canada decreased her ROW exports by 10 percent. Column 3 shows the forecasts if the United States increased exports by 10 percent and Canada simultaneously decreased hers by 10 percent. This last result would be a case where a good bit of the impact of the U.S. change would be offset by the Canadian change.

Analysis of a Demand Side Change

Table 5.7 shows the effect of changing feed grain prices by 50 percent for different countries. A cross elasticity of wheat for feed grains of .1 is assumed for the United States, Canada, Argentina, and Europe. A zero substitution elasticity is presumed for Australia and Japan. The four columns show the predicted effects if feed grain prices rose by 50 percent only in the country involved.

TABLE 5.5

Forecast Changes, by Flow and Total, from a 10 Percent Increase in Transport Costs
(percentage change)

	EU	JU	EC	JC	EA	JA	EG	Total
DUU	1.0	.4	.04	-.1	0	-.05	-.1	1.19
DEU	-15.5	8.5	3.7	-3.7	2.5	-2.6	.5	-6.6
DJU	6.4	-9.8	-3.3	3.7	-2.0	2.4	-.1	-2.7
DCC	.2	-.4	1.1	.7	-.04	-0	-.1	1.46
DEC	2.8	-3.9	-10.1	7.7	1.8	-1.9	.3	-3.3
DJC	-5.3	7.8	12.7	-14.8	-2.7	3.1	-.3	.5
DAA	1.5	-.3	.03	-.1	.4	.5	-.03	2.0
DEA	4.4	-6.2	4.1	-4.2	-16.0	13.3	.4	-4.2
DJA	-3.8	5.6	-3.0	3.3	9.5	-11.6	-.2	-.2
DGG	.01	-.09	-.1	.1	-.1	.1	1.2	1.12
DEG	-.2	1.2	1.8	-1.2	1.4	-1.0	-16.6	-14.6
DEE	—	—	—	—	—	—	—	—
DJJ	0	0	0	0	0	0	0	0
DPUU	-4.9	-2.1	-.2	.5	-.0	.3	.3	-6.11
DPEU	5.1	-2.1	-.2	.5	-.0	.3	.3	3.9
DPJU	-4.9	7.9	-.2	.5	-.0	.3	.3	3.9
DPCC	-1.0	2.0	-5.6	-3.3	.2	.03	.4	-7.27
DPEC	-1.0	2.0	4.4	-3.3	.2	.03	.4	2.7
DPJC	-1.0	2.0	-5.6	6.7	.2	.03	.4	2.7
DPAA	-1.6	2.7	-.3	.7	-3.8	-5.0	.3	-7.0
DPEA	-1.6	2.7	-.3	.7	6.1	-5.0	.3	2.9
DPJA	-1.6	2.7	-.3	.7	-3.8	5.0	.3	3.0
DPGG	-.04	.3	.4	-.3	.3	-.3	-4.0	-3.6
DPEG	-.04	.3	.4	-.3	.3	-.3	6.0	6.4
DPEE	-.1	.7	1.0	-.7	.8	-.6	.5	1.6
DPJJ	-2.8	4.6	-1.3	1.8	-.7	1.1	.3	3.0
SPU	-4.9	-2.1	-.2	.5	-.0	.3	.3	-6.1
SPC	-1.0	2.0	-5.6	-3.3	.2	.03	.4	-7.27
SPA	-1.6	2.7	-.3	.7	-3.8	-5.0	.3	-7.0
SPG	-.04	.3	.4	-.3	.3	-.3	-4.0	-3.6
SPE	-.1	.7	1.0	-.7	.8	-.6	.5	1.6
SPJ	-2.8	4.6	-1.3	1.8	-.7	1.1	.3	3.0

Source: Compiled by the authors.

TABLE 5.6

Forecast Changes from Changing Exogenous Exports
(percentage change)

	U.S. ROW Exports Increase 10 Percent	Canada ROW Exports Increase 10 Percent	Both Flows Increase 10 Percent
DUU	−3.6	.9	−2.7
DEU	−41.6	−.7	−42.3
DJU	−20.2	−5.2	−25.5
DCC	−1.1	3.0	1.9
DEC	−6.6	31.3	24.7
DJC	14.8	26.7	41.5
DAA	−.7	.5	−.2
DEA	−10.7	1.3	−9.4
DJA	10.7	−3.3	7.4
DGG	−.4	.6	.2
DEG	6.0	−8.1	−2.1
DEE	—	—	—
DJJ	0	0	0
DPUU	17.3	−4.5	12.8
DPEU	17.3	−4.5	12.8
DPJU	17.3	−4.5	12.8
DPCC	5.7	−15.1	−9.4
DPEC	5.7	−15.1	−9.4
DPJC	5.7	−15.1	−9.4
DPAA	7.0	−5.1	1.9
DPEA	7.0	−5.1	1.9
DPJA	7.0	−5.1	1.9
DPGG	1.5	−2.0	−.5
DPEG	1.5	−2.0	−.5
DPEE	3.5	−4.7	−1.2
DPJJ	10.6	−6.2	4.4
SPU	17.3	−4.5	12.8
SPC	5.7	−15.1	−9.4
SPA	7.0	−5.1	1.9
SPG	1.5	−2.0	−.5
SPE	3.5	−4.7	−1.2
SPJ	10.6	−6.2	4.4

Source: Compiled by the authors.

TABLE 5.7

Forecast Changes from a 50 Percent Increase in Feed Grain Prices
(percentage change)

	UU	CC	GG	EE
DUU	3.5	-.2	-.1	-1.0
DEU	-17.1	.1	.9	8.6
DJU	-8.3	1.1	-.1	-.9
DCC	-.5	4.4	-.1	-1.2
DEC	-2.73	-6.2	.5	5.2
DJC	6.06	-5.3	-.4	-4.3
DAA	-.3	-.1	-.1	-.5
DEA	-4.41	-.3	.7	6.9
DJA	4.41	.6	-.3	-2.5
DGG	.2	-.1	2.0	-1.0
DEG	2.48	1.6	-27.7	13.2
DEE	—	—	—	—
DJJ	0	0	0	0
DPUU	7.1	.9	.5	4.7
DPEU	7.1	.9	.5	4.7
DPJU	7.1	.9	.5	4.7
DPCC	2.3	3.0	.6	5.9
DPEC	2.3	3.0	.6	5.9
DPJC	2.3	3.0	.6	5.9
DPAA	2.9	1.0	.5	5.3
DPEA	2.9	1.0	.5	5.3
DPJA	2.9	1.0	.5	5.3
DPGG	.6	.4	10.0	3.2
DPEG	.6	.4	10.0	3.2
DPEE	1.4	.9	.8	9.3
DPJJ	4.3	1.2	.5	4.4
SPU	7.1	.9	.5	4.7
SPC	2.3	3.0	.6	5.9
SPA	2.9	1.0	.5	5.3
SPG	.6	.4	10.0	3.2
SPE	1.4	.9	.8	9.3
SPJ	4.3	1.2	.5	4.4

Source: Compiled by the authors.

TABLE 5.8

Exogenous Shifters Used in Forecasting Experiments
(percentage changes)

	1964/65 1965/66	1965/66 1966/67	1966/67 1967/68
Demand shift			
United States	−.64	−1.19	−2.26
Europe	.6	.24	−.97
Japan	1.38	1.87	2.17
Canada	1.02	1.47	.84
Europe	.6	.24	−.97
Japan	1.38	1.87	2.17
Australia	1.22	.21	.62
Europe	.6	.24	−.97
Japan	1.38	1.87	2.17
Argentina	−1.18	−.39	.54
Europe	.6	.24	−.97
Europe	.6	.24	−.97
Japan	1.38	1.87	2.17
Price difference			
UU	—	—	—
EU	−.26	−2.50	1.18
JU	2.43	1.48	2.59
CC	—	—	—
EC	−.39	−1.20	.67
JC	3.58	2.71	4.91
AA	—	—	—
EA	1.71	−3.33	−2.80
JA	5.27	.09	6.93
GG	—	—	—
EG	2.20	−3.97	.13
EE	—	—	—
JJ	—	—	—
Change in supply			
U	15.50	−12.02	−1.64
C	30.26	−10.07	−28.34
A	−30.81	40.41	−27.22
G	−9.18	−37.73	4.37
E	1.40	−6.32	3.34
J	3.40	−22.76	−5.42
Exogenous export ROW			
United States	9.96	−18.88	4.38
Canada	40.27	−5.66	−67.47
Australia	−16.55	26.25	−6.77
Argentina	87.88	−99.79	−89.20
Europe	2.94	−21.17	−3.53

1967/68 1968/69	1968/69 1969/70	1969/70 1970/71	1970/71 1971/72	1971/72 1972/73	1972/73 1973/74
-.23	-.03	1.87	-1.33	1.60	6.11
-.19	1.21	1.56	-1.62	3.07	6.0
2.23	2.04	1.88	1.56	1.75	.9
-1.83	-.04	3.50	-.25	4.17	11.3
-.19	1.21	1.56	-1.62	3.07	6.0
2.23	2.04	1.88	1.56	1.75	.9
-.24	.33	.53	.84	1.4	1.4
-.19	1.21	1.56	-1.62	3.07	6.0
2.23	2.04	1.88	1.56	1.75	.9
.11	-.99	-.74	-1.36	.68	4.2
-.19	1.21	1.56	-1.62	3.07	6.0
-.19	1.21	1.56	-1.62	3.07	6.0
2.23	2.04	1.88	1.56	1.75	.9
—	—	—	—	—	—
.1	3.1	-6.1	4.8	-15.8	-10.2
.96	10.62	-3.4	-14.03	-9.8	-38.3
—	—	—	—	—	—
-1.9	.2	-3.3	4.3	5.7	24.6
2.21	7.47	10.2	-14.53	8.6	12.7
—	—	—	—	—	—
0	4.8	1.6	3.9	10.7	41.8
-1.57	6.88	5.8	-6.52	16.3	29.0
—	—	—	—	—	—
.7	-.6	4.8	23.1	43.41	-8.5
—	—	—	—	—	—
—	—	—	—	—	—
-8.59	7.37	8.91	-1.27	27.99	-3.67
-8.41	12.90	13.86	11.51	10.00	-25.03
7.07	16.81	10.03	-11.19	-34.36	36.48
3.52	-4.13	-26.38	15.49	38.46	-61.25
16.32	7.38	-3.71	2.85	12.21	-10.37
4.24	-28.70	-46.10	-7.44	-42.76	-33.74
-39.53	20.52	4.69	-5.03	65.29	-8.0
-3.75	14.38	33.82	24.42	23.33	-40.8
-53.27	41.66	25.23	-15.83	-60.03	72.6
81.84	-24.98	-33.43	124.03	87.5	-76.7
7.07	40.50	-69.7	28.16	58.33	-33.0

Source: Compiled by the authors.

If the feed grain price went up by 50 percent everywhere, the total impact would involve the sum of these forecast changes plus the sum of the changes for the export flows. Such a total effect is not shown. (Note that any demand side shifter of 5 percent would yield the predictions in the table.)

FORECASTS

Flows

Table 5.8 contains the exogenous shifters used in the forecasting experiments. The first 13 rows are the demand shifters, the next 13 are exogenous price shifters, the next 6 are change in supply, and the last 5 are exogenous flows to the rest of the world. The forecast and actual percentage changes in the endogenous variables are shown in Table 5.9. Here the first 13 rows are the changes in flows of wheat, the next 13 are demand price changes, the next 6 are supply price changes, the last 5 simply repeat the changes in ROW exports.

The information in Tables 5.8 and 5.9 is in percentage changes. Since the absolute size of the different flows varies considerably, one can tell only about direction from these tables and not about magnitude. For information on magnitudes one needs to turn to Table 5.10. Here are shown for each of nine years three levels for each flow. The first column for each year is headed naive. This entry is simply last year's level for that flow, the second column is our forecast for that flow for that year based on the percentage change forecast. The third column is the actual magnitude of that flow for the year in question. One can now compare the forecast with the actual flow in terms of 1,000 metric-ton units.

In order to make some judgment about the forecasts, our estimates can be compared to the set of naive forecasts. The naive forecast simply says that in the absence of any structural information the best forecast for this year's flow is last year's flow.* One can thus ask the question: Are our forecasts more accurate than simply projecting last year's value forward a year? As will be seen, this question does not have a simple yes or no answer.

The flows under consideration are the endogenous flows of wheat, own consumption plus exports. These flows represent something less than one-third

---

*This is not the best naive forecast for a trending variable. In that case the procedure would be to apply the preceding year's rate of change to last year's level. With the possible exception of Japan's downward trending own production, there does not seem to be a pronounced trend in these flows. Despite a slight positive trend in world consumption of wheat, our endogenous flows do not have an obvious trend. The fact that wheat consumption has an animal feed dimension means that the fluctuations one observes can be considered as occurring around a mean value rather than a trend line for short time periods.

TABLE 5.9

Predicted and Actual Percentage Changes in Endogenous Variables

	1964/65 1965/66		1965/66 1966/67		1966/67 1967/68	
	Predicted	Actual	Predicted	Actual	Predicted	Actual
DUU	6.9	12.7	-.61	-8.3	-6.3	-6.1
DEU	130.0	89.9	-20.7	-15.1	-36.2	-27.1
DJU	89.0	16.1	-49.4	9.4	33.5	4.0
DCC	3.2	6.3	2.1	-1.0	-1.0	7.9
DEC	52.6	-10.6	-24.1	6.1	-3.8	-16.0
DJC	7.8	-10.9	-52.6	23.1	57.4	-38.4
DAA	-4.9	-5.3	10.1	-3.5	-8.7	9.5
DEA	-168.3	25.6	272.4	-22.7	-243.0	33.7
DJA	-211.2	-19.9	244.3	17.1	-199.2	34.7
DGG	-24.6	-1.0	6.6	7.0	11.1	7.7
DEG	-222.1	-37.8	45.0	-40.8	131.3	-46.1
DEE	1.13	-1.0	-2.7	-3.7	2.8	5.7
DJJ	3.4	-1.0	-22.8	-19.6	-5.4	-11.0
DPUU	-36.8	2.5	-2.8	13.9	19.7	-15.1
DPEU	-37.0	-5.9	-5.3	8.2	20.9	-5.0
DPJU	-34.3	-16.5	-1.3	12.6	22.3	-6.3
DPCC	-10.8	.7	-3.0	6.1	9.4	-8.7
DPEC	-11.2	1.0	-4.2	2.9	10.1	-5.2
DPJC	-7.2	-9.2	-.2	5.5	14.3	-4.4
DPAA	60.7	4.2	-99.6	2.2	93.2	5.6

(continued)

67

(Table 5.9 continued)

	Predicted	Actual	Predicted	Actual	Predicted	Actual
DPEA	62.4	3.6	-103.0	3.2	90.4	2.7
DPJA	66.0	-9.4	-99.5	5.1	100.1	-4.4
DPGG	78.1	-5.5	-23.2	5.8	-35.1	5.8
DPEG	80.3	-1.3	-27.2	6.5	-35.0	-3.6
DPEE	6.0	.9	-11.3	5.5	7.9	-7.6
DPJJ	-5.8	0	-10.2	0	35.2	-1.0
SPU	-36.8	2.5	-2.8	13.9	19.7	-15.1
SPC	-10.8	.7	-3.0	6.1	9.4	-8.7
SPA	60.7	4.2	-99.6	2.2	93.2	5.6
SPG	78.1	-5.5	-23.2	5.8	-35.1	5.8
SPE	6.0	.9	-11.3	5.5	7.9	-7.6
SPJ	-5.8	0	-10.2	0	35.2	-1.0
DRU	10.0	10.0	-18.9	-18.9	4.4	4.4
DRC	40.3	40.3	-5.7	-5.7	-67.5	-67.5
DRA	-16.6	-16.6	26.2	26.2	-6.8	-6.8
DRG	87.9	87.9	-99.8	-99.8	-89.7	-89.7
DRE	2.9	2.9	-26.3	-26.3	7.0	7.0
	1967/68		1968/69		1969/70	
	1968/69		1969/70		1970/71	
DUU	11.6	14.9	1.6	4.8	6.8	-.1
DEU	52.2	11.2	-5.1	-13.7	32.0	59.4
DJU	13.2	-18.9	2.4	25.7	44.9	18.9
DCC	4.7	-6.4	2.6	13.7	6.6	-5.8

68

DEC	-16.1	-6.7	20.2	-9.9	-2.0	25.6
DJC	-64.9	12.7	26.6	-15.5	-21.6	-3.7
DAA	10.2	-17.2	.4	6.3	1.8	10.2
DEA	193.0	18.6	-30.6	25.9	-24.0	37.2
DJA	160.2	60.8	-8.6	-15.7	-15.7	-17.7
DGG	-6.1	-7.7	1.9	7.5	11.5	-2.4
DEG	-184.1	33.7	12.0	-34.6	49.9	10.8
DEE	15.9	2.6	4.4	6.3	11.5	-3.7
DJ	4.24	9.1	-28.7	-28.1	46.1	-46.1
DPUU	-57.6	-8.5	-7.8	-.6	-23.9	3.1
DPEU	-57.4	-.2	-4.7	-2.6	-30.0	0
DPJU	-56.6	-1.1	2.2	-5.4	-27.3	-6.7
DPCC	-32.8	.3	-13.3	6.4	-15.3	3.3
DPEC	-34.7	-3.8	-13.1	-2.1	-18.6	0
DPJC	-30.6	-2.3	-5.9	-4.9	-5.1	6.7
DPAA	-104.4	3.3	-1.0	.1	-12.9	-3.0
DPEA	-104.4	4.0	3.8	-3.0	-11.3	0
DPJA	-106.0	-2.3	5.9	-4.9	-7.1	-6.7
DPGG	20.6	-6.1	-9.8	-4.7	-40.7	0
DPEG	21.3	-2.1	-10.4	-3.7	-35.9	0
DPEE	-45.5	8.6	-7.9	5.5	-23.2	-5.5
DPJJ	-53.6	-1.0	12.6	0	3.0	-6.3
SPU	-57.6	-8.5	-7.8	-.6	-23.9	.7
SPC	-32.8	.3	-13.3	6.4	-15.3	.5
SPA	-104.4	3.3	-1.0	.1	-12.9	-3.8
SPG	-20.6	-6.1	-9.8	-4.7	-40.7	0

(continued)

69

(Table 5.9 continued)

	Predicted	Actual	Predicted	Actual	Predicted	Actual
SPE	-45.5	8.6	-7.9	5.5	-23.2	.2
SPJ	-53.6	-1.0	12.6	0	3.0	-1.8
DRU	-39.5	-39.5	20.5	20.5	4.7	4.7
DRC	-3.3	-3.3	14.4	14.4	33.8	33.8
DRA	-53.3	-53.3	41.7	41.7	25.2	25.2
DRG	81.8	81.8	-25.0	-25.0	-140.8	-140.8
DRE	19.0	19.0	22.9	22.9	-69.7	-69.7
	1970/71		1971/72		1972/73	
	1971/72		1972/73		1973/74	
DUU	-3.2	10.7	3.6	-8.3	-4.5	-4.7
DEU	13.3	-56.0	54.9	44.5	-21.3	-.6
DJU	14.6	-26.9	40.2	42.4	2.9	-9.6
DCC	-2.8	3.1	5.8	-1.0	8.9	-6.1
DEC	4.3	-18.8	-14.1	-21.0	-7.7	-6.0
DJC	5.6	29.7	-19.5	-1.7	-32.1	21.5
DAA	-.7	3.6	2.9	18.6	3.9	.6
DEA	-3.3	-73.0	-9.5	-53.9	50.2	0
DJA	-27.2	56.4	-23.0	-68.6	28.4	-41.2
DGG	4.4	3.2	22.5	17.5	-36.9	-28.4
DEG	43.9	-41.3	67.1	6.0	-283.9	1.3
DEE	-12.9	9.4	6.8	6.0	-5.3	-5.7
DJJ	-7.4	-10.0	-42.8	-51.3	-33.7	-33.7
DPUU	9.2	1.3	-9.6	34.2	51.2	59.1
DPEU	14.0	-6.5	-25.4	32.4	41.0	0

DPJU	−4.9	−4.2	−19.4	40.9	12.9	0
DPCC	12.7	−3.4	−8.1	34.3	12.3	15.7
DPEC	17.0	−2.3	−2.4	33.9	36.1	0
DPJC	−1.9	−5.3	.5	37.8	24.6	0
DPAA	15.6	2.2	−14.6	3.3	−24.5	0
DPEA	19.5	−9.6	−3.9	40.1	17.3	0
DPJA	9.1	−5.3	1.7	28.3	4.5	
DPGG	−19.4	8.4	−72.8	33.1	137.0	
DPEG	3.8	0	−29.4	40.0	128.5	
DPEE	22.7	−16.8	−9.4	47.1	35.8	0
DPJJ	2.5	0	8.3	2.6	25.1	5.4
SPU	9.2	1.3	−9.6	34.2	51.2	59.1
SPC	12.7	−3.4	−8.1	34.3	12.3	15.7
SPA	15.6	2.2	−14.6	3.3	24.5	−9.0
SPG	−19.4	8.4	−72.8	33.1	137.0	
SPE	22.7	0	−9.4	47.1	35.8	0
SPJ	2.5	0	8.3	2.6	25.1	5.4
DRU	−5.0	−5.0	65.3	65.3	−2.0	−2.0
DRC	24.4	24.4	23.3	23.3	−40.8	−40.8
DRA	−15.8	−15.8	−60.0	−60.0	72.6	72.6
DRG	124.8	124.8	87.5	87.5	−76.7	−76.7
DRE	37.8	37.8	53.4	53.4	−33.0	−33.0

Source: Actual price data were obtained from the following sources supplemented by unpublished data from the U.S. Department of Agriculture: U.S. Department of Agriculture, *Agricultural Statistics*, U.S. Government Printing Office, Washington, D.C., 1976; Canadian Wheat Board, *Annual Report*, Winnipeg, various issues; Bureau of Agricultural Economics, *Wheat: Situation and Outlook*, Canberra, 1975; Statistical Office of the European Communities, *Yearbook of Agricultural Statistics*, Luxembourg, 1976.

TABLE 5.10

Two Forecasts and Actual Flows of Wheat
(metric tons)

	Naive	Ours	Actual	Naive	Ours	Actual	Naive	Ours	Actual
		1965/66			1966/67			1967/68	
DUU	17,486	18,692	19,876	19,876	19,757	18,442	18,442	17,280	17,606
DEU	1,062	2,443	2,796	2,796	2,217	2,404	2,404	1,534	1,832
DJU	1,654	3,126	1,943	1,943	983	2,135	2,135	2,850	2,225
DCC	4,008	4,136	4,270	4,270	4,360	4,229	4,229	4,187	4,557
DEC	3,719	5,675	3,344	3,344	2,538	3,556	3,556	3,421	3,030
DJC	1,433	1,545	1,285	1,285	609	1,620	1,620	2,543	1,098
DAA	2,659	2,528	2,522	2,522	2,774	2,435	2,435	2,223	2,678
DEA	568	—	735	735	1,900	585	585	—	822
DJA	443	—	363	363	880	431	431	—	612
DGG	3,730	2,812	3,705	3,705	3,949	3,975	3,975	4,412	4,295
DEG	1,812	—	1,236	1,236	1,792	817	817	1,634	511
DEE	24,174	24,440	23,481	23,481	21,908	23,355	23,355	24,009	24,362
DJ	1,164	1,204	1,153	1,153	947	947	947	848	848

	Naive	Ours	Actual	Naive	Ours	Actual	Naive	Ours	Actual
		1968/69			1969/70			1970/71	
DUU	17,606	19,631	19,986	19,986	20,306	20,912	20,912	22,355	20,902
DEU	1,832	2,858	2,048	2,048	1,915	1,785	1,785	2,360	3,292
DJU	2,225	2,470	1,837	1,837	1,898	2,382	2,382	3,428	2,878
DCC	4,557	4,798	4,291	4,291	4,402	4,924	4,924	5,264	4,648
DEC	3,030	2,463	2,833	2,833	3,400	2,567	2,567	2,475	3,319

		1971/72			1972/73			1973/74	
DJC	1,098	468	1,247	1,247	1,559	1,068	1,068	874	1,029
DAA	2,678	2,946	2,254	2,254	2,263	2,399	2,399	2,447	2,658
DEA	822	2,000	991	991	694	1,286	1,286	964	1,873
DJA	612	1,579	1,147	1,147	1,036	980	980	845	821
DGG	4,295	3,999	3,976	3,976	4,091	4,286	4,286	4,809	4,184
DEG	511	—	718	718	767	506	506	724	564
DEE	—	—	—	29,617	30,920	31,919	31,919	35,590	30,608
DJJ	848	929	929	929	646	646	646	439	439

		1971/72			1972/73			1973/74	
DUU	20,902	19,982	23,269	23,269	24,107	21,419	21,419	20,435	20,439
DEU	3,292	3,983	1,773	1,773	2,730	2,788	2,788	2,194	2,473
DJU	2,878	3,269	2,195	2,195	3,073	3,377	3,377	3,475	3,067
DCC	4,648	4,467	4,796	4,796	5,074	4,764	4,764	5,187	4,482
DEC	3,319	3,518	2,749	2,749	2,361	2,477	2,477	2,286	2,333
DJC	1,029	1,080	1,388	1,388	1,117	1,364	1,364	940	1,692
DAA	2,658	2,618	2,706	2,706	2,784	3,260	3,260	3,387	3,279
DEA	1,873	1,901	871	871	788	501	501	753	—
DJA	821	534	1,466	1,466	1,129	717	717	921	472
DGG	4,184	4,268	4,320	4,320	5,292	5,151	5,151	3,462	4,130
DEG	564	914	352	352	587	374	374	—	379
DEE	30,608	26,935	33,400	33,400	35,671	35,919	35,919	34,015	34,900
DJJ	439	397	397	397	235	235	235	202	202

Source: Actual price data were obtained from the following sources supplemented by unpublished data from the U.S. Department of Agriculture: U.S. Department of Agriculture, *Agricultural Statistics*, U.S. Government Printing Office, Washington, D.C., 1976; Canadian Wheat Board, *Annual Report*, Winnipeg, various issues; Bureau of Agricultural Economics, *Wheat: Situation and Outlook*, Canberra, 1975; Statistical Office of the European Communities, *Yearbook of Agricultural Statistics*, Luxembourg, 1976.

of the world's wheat production, but they represent a much more sizable fraction of the wheat that is available to the world's markets in any given year. A large part of the world's wheat is produced and consumed in the same area. For most of the period considered, flows to Asia, other than Japan, are the notable omission from the endogenous flows. The USSR is essentially a special case. The import demands of the Soviets are extremely volatile and of large magnitude when they occur. Questions of accuracy, then, really concern the endogenous, essentially stable, flows of own consumption and traditional export markets.

Two quite different questions can be asked of the data in Table 5.10. One is to consider each forecast flow individually. The more accurate forecast, then, is the one closer to the actual result. The aggregate measure for this performance is to add up the discrepancies for the two forecasts and compare the totals. This measure is shown in Table 5.11 as the sum of absolute errors for the naive and our forecast. Each number is the amount in thousand metric tons that forecasts for all countries miss the target in the year shown.

The alternative is to consider each year as an experiment, and to ask how well each type of forecast was able to predict the allocation of all flows considered jointly. The measure for this is the algebraic sum of the discrepancies. The rationale for this measure is that for a particular exporter the model might overshoot one flow and undershoot another. For some purposes this would be a better forecast than one that consistently was over or under for all flows.

TABLE 5.11

Discrepancies between Actual Flows and Naive Forecasts and Actual Flows and Our Forecasts (thousand metric tons)

	Sum of Absolute Errors		Sum of Signed Errors	
	Naive	Ours	Naive	Ours
1965/66	6,877	8,987	−2,787	−809
1966/67	3,962	8,424	1,788	620
1967/68	5,267	6,785	455	217
1968/69	5,331	6,328	−2,143	1,884
1969/70	6,526	5,304	−3,786	−1,762
1970/71	5,663	7,439	−1,655	1,647
1971/72	10,523	17,106	−2,467	−5,816
1972/73	9,582	5,500	−2,664	2,602
1973/74	5,202	5,436	4,498	−698

Source: Compiled by the authors.

TABLE 5.12

Sums of Flow Discrepancies, United States and Canada, 1965/66–1973/74

Flow	Aggregate		Signed	
	Naive	Ours	Naive	Ours
UU	13,173	11,258	−2,953	−296
EU	7,533	5,257	−1,411	1,043
JU	4,165	6,212	−1,403	2,333
CC	2,288	3,623	−454	915
EC	3,314	6,718	2,032	1,927
JC	2,272	5,448	−269	−385

Source: Compiled by the authors.

The naive model performs better in terms of number of years for the absolute deviation. On the other hand, the structural forecasting model does better in terms of the signed deviations. One way to interpret this result is that our economic structure allocates a given array of supply changes better than no structure, even though the observed results on the average could not be considered outstanding forecasts.* Putting it another way, our model does a better job of allocating the endogenous wheat flows than the absence of a model.

Another aggregation of forecast discrepancies is to sum through time the discrepancies for a naive and our model.† Table 5.12 shows the sums of discrepancies through time (1965/66 through 1973/74) of a naive and our model for the United States and Canada.

Again both an absolute and algebraic sum are shown. The absolute sum treats over- and underestimates the same. The algebraic sum says that an underestimate in one year has an offsetting effect on an overestimate in another year. The results are somewhat ambiguous. Our model is better for the U.S. own flow, but poorer for two Canadian flows. Our model overestimated all flows but two, while the naive model underestimated all but one flow. At the moment we put no particular interpretation on these results.

---

*Note that in our framework these forecasts are not really stochastic in nature. Therefore the deviations calculated cannot be used for any probability statements or hypothesis tests. A year's observation is simply one estimate of a set of mutually dependent variables (see next footnote).

†These forecast discrepancies are more similar to those of econometric models that consider forecasts to be stochastic variables. Again, we are really treating the structure as deterministic and make no probability statements about forecast capability.

TABLE 5.13

Two Forecasts and Actual Prices for Major Exporters

	Naive	Ours	Actual	Naive	Ours	Actual
		1964/65–1965/66			1965/66–1966/67	
SPU	64.67	40.87	59.52	59.52	57.85	67.24
SPC	66.63	59.43	67.19	67.19	65.17	71.09
SPA	58.32	93.72	58.69	58.69	.23	63.02
SPG	58.47	104.08	55.32	55.32	42.49	58.65
		1966/67–1967/68			1967/68–1968/69	
SPU	67.24	80.49	62.83	62.83	26.95	63.20
SPC	71.09	77.77	65.60	65.60	42.31	68.64
SPA	63.02		58.23	58.23		57.98
SPG	58.65	38.06	62.18	62.18	76.73	58.48
		1968/69–1969/70			1969/70–1970/71	
SPU	63.20	58.08	57.32	57.32	58.47	62.83
SPC	68.64	59.72	64.28	64.28	65.95	67.63
SPA	57.98	57.63	53.93	53.93	51.13	57.63
SPG	58.48	51.11	55.78	55.78	79.76	56.59
		1970/71–1971/72			1971/72–1972/73	
SPU	62.83	72.13	61.73	61.73	56.42	91.86
SPC	67.63	79.87	64.63	64.63	59.39	91.99
SPA	57.63	71.29	57.74	57.74	49.31	90.90
SPG	56.59	50.31	61.55	61.55	11.08	85.98

Source: Actual price data were obtained from the following sources supplemented by unpublished data from the U.S. Department of Agriculture: U.S. Department of Agriculture, *Agricultural Statistics*, U.S. Government Printing Office, Washington, D.C., 1976; Canadian Wheat Board, *Annual Report*, Winnipeg, various issues; Bureau of Agricultural Economics, *Wheat: Situation and Outlook*, Canberra, 1975; Statistical Office of the European Communities, *Yearbook of Agricultural Statistics*, Luxembourg, 1976.

Prices

The forecast prices are generally poorer than the forecast flows. The forecast prices and the actual (export) prices for the four major exporters for 1965/66 through 1973/74 are shown in Table 5.13. Quite good forecasts are obtained for 1969/70, 1970/71, and 1973/74. For the latter two years the improvement seems due to our investment in improving our knowledge of policy shifts and other exogenous changes. This process of improvement is shown in some detail in Chapter 7, which discusses the 1973/74 experience at length. Instead of investing in seeking more accurate exogenous shift data, we have decided to let these later years speak for themselves and not try to explain the 1960s. The following section should help clarify the data problems.

SENSITIVITY OF THE MODEL

There is an implicit identification problem embedded in examining the accuracy of our forecasts. Is poor accuracy the result of the parameters, for example, demand elasticities or the quality of the data? In the second case there is a two-part problem—the quality of the data for the exogenous shifters and the data we are trying to forecast are both subject to question. One mode of attack is to concentrate on a few years and vary some changes in a systematic manner to try to identify the source of what appears at first blush to be erratic changes in forecasts from relatively small exogenous changes. This systematic examination of particular changes is taken up in Chapter 7. The sensitivity of results to different parameter values has been discussed earlier in the current chapter.

Another way of analyzing the sensitivity of the model is to examine the nature of the model itself. The model can be written as

$$XY = A$$

where Y is a vector of endogenous variables to be predicted, X is the matrix of parameters of the demand equations and information on market shares, and A is the vector of exogenous shifts.

Solving for Y involves inverting X and multiplying X^{-1} by A. Each element in the inverse can be thought of as an impact multiplier in a reduced form. That is, to predict a particular Y, say Y_1, you multiply the vector A by the first row in X^{-1}. Call the elements of this row X^{ij}. Each of these elements is the partial derivative of Y_1 with respect to an element of A. In general each element of X^{-1} can be written as

$$X^{ij} = \frac{\partial Y_i}{\partial A_j}$$

The interpretation of these elements is that other things being held constant a change in Y_i that is due to a given change in an element of A is given by X^{ij}. In our model the first endogenous variable is the U.S. own consumption (DUU in our terminology), call this Y_1. The first shifter in A is the demand shifter for the United States made up of income and population changes, plus the change in feed grain prices times the appropriate elasticity, call this A_1. If one wants to ask what impact a 1 percent change in this shifter has on U.S. consumption of wheat, one can look at X^{11} (the element in the first row and column of X^{-1}). For the change 1969/70 to 1970/71 and the basic elasticities of the model this number happens to be 1.87. This means a 1 percent change in demand shifters would increase U.S. consumption by 1.87 percent in the absence of any other changes. (A more complete explanation of the multipliers is in the Appendix to this chapter.)

To get some idea of how changes get transmitted through the model we can look at the most important "multipliers." Since the most troublesome predictions have been price changes, let us examine one change in detail. Take the U.S. supply price change forecast. That forecast is found from multiplying row 27 in the inverse matrix times the exogenous shift vector. This row and the shift vector for 1969/70 to 1970/71 are written out in Table 5.14. As can be seen in the table, the biggest multipliers on the price variable are the own change in supply, the own demand shifter, and the exogenous export to ROW. It is interesting to note that a supply change of 8.9 percent observed in that year would lead to a forecast change in the price of −37.4 percent. The interrelationships in the model, along with the other exogenous shifters, more than offset this predicted price increase in this particular case. The forecast price change is an increase of approximately 2 percent, quite close to the actual real change of 1 percent.

Another instructive example is also included in this price forecast. The interrelationships of the model are such that a transport cost change is shared by both shippers and receivers, so that a transport cost decrease tends to raise the U.S. supply price (as the demand curve is shifted out) and to lower the demand price abroad. The impact, for instance, of a change in the United States to Japan transport cost is −.33 (16th entry in line 27).

The years 1969 and 1970 had quite volatile transport cost changes. There were marked trends in both years so that when the annual averages (on a July to June basis) are compared, some fairly strange observations result. For instance, ocean freight rates from the Gulf to Japan fell by 27 percent, implying a 3.4 percent decrease in the Japanese wheat price, while rates from the Pacific Northwest rose by 6.4 percent, implying an 8 percent increase in wheat prices in Japan.* Thus even though the impact multiplier for the United States to Japan

---

*We have used the Gulf shipping rates throughout, so the 3.4 decrease in the shift shows in Table 5.14.

TABLE 5.14

Impact Multipliers and Shift Vector for the Forecast of U.S. Supply Price Change, 1969/70-1970/71

Exogenous Shifter	Shift Vector	Multiplier from Row 27
Demand shift		
United States	1.87	2.35
Europe	1.56	.08
Japan	1.88	.27
Canada	3.50	.15
Europe	1.56	.08
Japan	1.88	.03
Australia	.53	.09
Europe	1.56	.05
Japan	1.88	.04
Argentina	−.74	.05
Europe	1.56	.01
Europe	1.56	.63
Japan	1.88	.05
Price difference		
UU	—	−.48
EU	−6.1	−.18
JU	−3.4	−.33
CC	—	—
EC	−3.3	−.08
JC	10.2	.11
AA	—	−.01
EA	1.6	−.07
JA	5.8	.08
GG	—	−.02
EG	4.8	.02
EE	—	.00
JJ	—	0
Change in supply		
U	8.9	−4.2
C	13.9	−.44
A	10.0	−.40
G	−26.4	−.08
E	−3.7	−.78
J	−46.1	−.05
Exogenous export ROW		
United States	4.7	1.5
Canada	33.8	.18
Australia	25.2	.22
Argentina	−33.4	.02
Europe	−69.7	.15

Source: Compiled by the authors.

price change is only -.33, and the freight rate change is only one component of the price change, this difference leads to a forecast discrepancy of the U.S. wheat price of plus .25 percent to minus 1 percent. The sensitivity is to an exogenous change and not to any particular property of the model that we have built in.

This sensitivity of the model to the exogenous shifters used should not be interpreted as a drawback of the model. The wheat market itself can be very volatile. It is because of this potential that governments have intervened in that market and have introduced some of the institutions we are trying to model. Wheat, after all, is a commodity with a very small elasticity of demand. Small changes in supply would lead to fairly substantial changes in prices, in the absence of any intervention.

APPENDIX: A MATHEMATICAL STATEMENT OF THE SYSTEM SOLUTION AND THE IMPACT MULTIPLIERS

The System

The set of equations that yields solution values for endogenous values is as follows: $XY = A$ or

$$
\begin{bmatrix}
{}_fE_f & -{}_fI_f & {}_fO_n & {}_fO_n \\
{}_fI_f & {}_fO_f & -{}_fU_n & {}_fO_n \\
{}_nO_f & {}_nM_f & {}_nO_n & {}_nD_n \\
{}_nO_F & {}_nO_f & {}_nO_n & {}_nI_n
\end{bmatrix}
\begin{bmatrix}
DPIJ \\
DIJ \\
DSPJ \\
R
\end{bmatrix}
=
\begin{bmatrix}
-DSHIFT \\
PSHIFT \\
DSJ \\
R
\end{bmatrix}
$$

Dimensions are indicated where f is the number of active flows and n the number of countries or regions included in the model.

$$X^{-1}$$

Partitioned inversion of the X matrix results in the following solution for the endogenous Y vector:

$$
\begin{array}{l}
\text{DPIJ} \\[6pt]
\text{DIJ} \\[6pt]
\text{DSPJ} \\[6pt]
\text{R}
\end{array}
=
\begin{bmatrix}
U(MEU)^{-1}M & I-U(MEU)^{-1}ME & U(MEU)^{-1} & -U(MEU)^{-1}D \\[6pt]
EU(MEU)^{-1}M-I & E-EU(MEU)^{-1}ME & EU(MEU)^{-1} & -EU(MEU)^{-1}D \\[6pt]
(MEU)^{-1}M & -(MEU)^{-1}ME & (MEU)^{-1} & -(MEU)^{-1}D \\[6pt]
0 & 0 & 0 & I
\end{bmatrix}
\begin{bmatrix}
-\text{DSHIFT} \\[6pt]
\text{PSHIFT} \\[6pt]
\text{DS} \\[6pt]
\text{R}
\end{bmatrix}
$$

At first inspection, one sees that all submatrixes of the inverse are related by the matrix $(MEU)^{-1}$ A closer examination of $(MEU)^{-1}$ and the structure of the other submatrixes of X^{-1} should lead to a greater understanding of the factors contributing to the magnitudes of the impact multipliers.

For thus purpose consider a three-country world composed of U, C, E. Assume U and C export to one another, that both export to E, and that E exports to no one; with intracountry flows, this is a total of seven flows. The E, M, and U matrixes follow:

$$
_7E_7 =
\begin{bmatrix}
\eta^U_{UU} & 0 & 0 & 0 & \eta^U_{UC} & 0 & 0 \\[6pt]
0 & \eta^C_{UU} & 0 & \eta^C_{UC} & 0 & 0 & 0 \\[6pt]
0 & 0 & \eta^E_{UU} & 0 & 0 & \eta^E_{UC} & \eta^E_{UE} \\[6pt]
0 & \eta^C_{CU} & 0 & \eta^C_{CC} & 0 & 0 & 0 \\[6pt]
\eta^U_{CU} & 0 & 0 & 0 & \eta^U_{CC} & 0 & 0 \\[6pt]
0 & 0 & \eta^E_{CU} & 0 & 0 & \eta^E_{CC} & \eta^E_{CE} \\[6pt]
0 & 0 & \eta^E_{EU} & 0 & 0 & \eta^E_{EC} & \eta^E_{EE}
\end{bmatrix}
$$

$$
_3M_7 =
\begin{bmatrix}
M^U_U & M^U_C & M^U_E & 0 & 0 & 0 & 0 \\[6pt]
0 & 0 & 0 & M^C_C & M^C_U & M^C_E & 0 \\[6pt]
0 & 0 & 0 & 0 & 0 & 0 & M^E_E
\end{bmatrix}
$$

$$
_7U_3 \; = \;
\begin{bmatrix}
w_U^U & 0 & 0 \\[6pt]
w_C^U & 0 & 0 \\[6pt]
w_E^U & 0 & 0 \\[6pt]
0 & w_C^C & 0 \\[6pt]
0 & w_U^C & 0 \\[6pt]
0 & w_E^C & 0 \\[6pt]
0 & 0 & w_E^E
\end{bmatrix}
$$

η_{ij}^k = elasticity of demand in k for i's grain with respect to the price of j's grain,

m_i^j = the share in j's exports that i occupies,

$$
MEU \; = \;
\begin{bmatrix}
\sum_i m_i^U w_i^U \, \eta_{UU}^i & \sum_i m_i^U w_i^C \, \eta_{UC}^i & m_E^U w_E^E \, \eta_{UE}^E \\[10pt]
\sum_i m_i^C w_i^U \, \eta_{CU}^i & \sum_i m_i^C w_i^C \, \eta_{CC}^i & m_E^C w_E^E \, \eta_{CE}^E \\[10pt]
m_E^E w_E^U \, \eta_{EU}^E & m_E^E w_{EC}^E \, \eta_{EC}^E & m_E^E w_E^E \, \eta_{EE}^E
\end{bmatrix}
$$

Consider the entry in cell 1, 1 in MEU. This is the weighted sum of the demand elasticities in each of the three countries for U's wheat with respect to the price of U's wheat in each country. A change in U's supply price will operate through these elasticities, but in order to determine the effect on U's grain demanded this change must first be dampened by a factor indicating the importance of U's supply price in i's demand price (w_i^U). If the resultant change in quantity demanded is weighted by m_i^U, and we assume shifts in price and demand and changes in ROW are zero, we then have the change in U's supply that must result to satisfy this demand. That is,

$$
\frac{\partial(DSJ)}{\partial(DSPJ)} = \sum_i m_i^j w_i^j \eta_{jj}^i
$$

If supply changes are exogenous, as in our case, we may ask the question, How does a given supply change affect supply price? We are asking for a price flexibility so we do not simply take the reciprocal of the above expression but rewrite our subsystem as

$$DSPJ = (MEU)^{-1} DSJ$$

the i, j element of $(MEU)^{-1}$ is $\frac{\partial(DSPI)}{\partial(DSJ)}$ and takes into account the effects of all cross elasticities; this is the submatrix in cell 3, 3 of X^{-1}.

If demand, price, and ROW shifts are not zero, the remaining submatrixes in row 3 of X^{-1} will indicate their effect on a given supply price. In the trial run for wheat for 1969/70 through 1970/71 percentage changes in exports to ROW had large effects on supply prices.

$$\frac{\partial(DSPJ)}{\partial(R)} = -(MEU)^{-1} D$$

Since D is a diagonal matrix with export shares down the diagonal, $-(MEU)^{-1}D$ is simply the elements of $(MEU)^{-1}$ multiplied by the negative of an export share. For example, we had

$$\frac{\partial(DSPU)}{\partial(DSU)} = -4.2$$

$$\frac{\partial(DSPU)}{\partial(RU)} = (-4.2)(-\frac{U\text{'s exports to ROW}}{U\text{'s consumption + total exports}})$$

$$= (-4.2)(-.36) = 1.5.$$

This indicates the only way to reduce the effect of these multipliers is to make more of the world endogenous, thereby reducing the value of the elements of D.

One final note concerns the "constant share" aspect of the model. The limitations imposed by this are very evident in the structure of the impact multipliers. Both M and D, which occur everywhere in X^{-1}, are last period's export shares and as they change during the forecast period the multipliers can be expected to change.

6

FURTHER APPLICATIONS
OF THE MODEL:
COARSE GRAINS
AND RICE

This chapter applies the world trade model to coarse grains and rice. For current purposes, coarse grains are taken to be Standard International Trade Classification numbers 043 (barley), 044 (maize), and 045 (cereals). The following seven countries and one region will be included in the application of the model: United States (U), Canada (C), Argentina (G), Australia (A), South Africa (F), Thailand (T), Japan (J), and the nine members of the European Economic Community (E). In the past this group has accounted for close to 100 percent of exports and 55 percent of imports of coarse grains.

THE COARSE GRAIN TRADE MODEL

The fundamental distinction between the wheat and rice models and that for coarse grains is found in the market expansion portion of the demand side of the model. Coarse grains are primarily a feed for livestock. For an importer, the relative movement of c.i.f. prices continues to be the mechanism by which import shares are determined. However, the size of the market no longer depends on the direct coarse grain purchases of ultimate consumers; it is mainly derived from the demand for feed by livestock producers and the demand for meat and other livestock products by ultimate consumers.

Wheat and rice may be treated as final products directly entering a consumer's utility function. Demand theory says that quantity demanded of a product depends on its own price, prices of related goods, income, and population. The utilization of these same variables for coarse grains will result in a misspecification of the demand equations.

Since coarse grains are predominantly used as feed, the above variables may be used to explain demand for livestock slaughter. The supply of slaughter depends on the price received, the cost of inputs, and the available capital stock, namely livestock inventory carryin. The slaughter decision is simultaneously a livestock inventory carryout decision; the two variables share a joint production relationship. Demand for coarse grains is derived from the joint production decision, hence it depends on own price, slaughter price, prices of related feeds, and livestock carryin. The structure (which is only one of many conceivable structures) contains a livestock slaughter demand equation, a joint slaughter and inventory supply equation, a coarse grain demand equation, and a livestock inventory identity. Coarse grain supply is taken to be exogenous.

From this structure the reduced form equation—which relates coarse grain demand to real income, population, own price, related feed prices, and livestock carryin—mainly differs from that for wheat or rice in the inclusion of the livestock variable. Coarse grain quantity and price remain constant elasticity of substitution index functions of own consumption and imported quantities and own price and import prices. The theoretical derivation of the coarse grain demand functions is similar to that of wheat outlined in Chapter 4. A two-step optimization procedure is again employed. The main difference is that the first stage is now a profit maximizing condition of feeders of grain rather than a utility maximization condition for consumers.

As in the case of wheat, direct estimation of the parameters for the demand side of the model presents difficulties. In the experiments described in the next section, elasticities from previous studies for various regions are used as the basic elasticities. Even with this expedient the coarse grain model presents problems on the demand side.*

We are again presenting the short-run forecasting capability of this kind of model. In the case of wheat, income effects are negligible in a calendar-year context. The derived demand nature of feed grains means that demand side shifters from income effects must be taken into account. In a long-run framework, both income and livestock variables would enter the reduced-form equation for feed grain quantity. In our short-run modeling effort, neither income nor livestock numbers was satisfactory, in a statistical sense, as a demand shifter. Consequently, a trend consumption variable was constructed. This variable is the percentage change between last year's actual consumption and this year's predicted consumption of feed grains, where the predicted value is obtained from a consumption on time regression. These regression results are shown in Table 6.1.

---

*At the time of writing, Keith Collins of North Carolina State University was nearing completion of a study that does in fact provide statistical estimates of feed-livestock sectors in the endogenous regions of the coarse grain model. These results will be incorporated in a trade model and will be published elsewhere.

TABLE 6.1

Regression of Consumption on Time, 1960–74

Dependent Variable Total Consumption	Intercept	Trend	DT*	DF*
U	118506.78	1792.33 (3.10)		
C	9576.65	434.35 (7.57)		
G	4128.05	258.48 (4.22)		
A	1753.10	92.88 (5.11)		
F	3199.44	217.00 (14.11)		−401.90 (−2.44)
F	3340.10	189.63 (15.98)		
T	−62.40	35.98 (10.92)	−116.56 (−3.86)	
T	−141.10	37.02 (8.13)		
E	52017.35	1593.94 (21.11)		
J	3229.73	688.74 (25.89)		

*For some years for Thailand and South Africa consumption figures were for corn only; DT and DF are dummy variables taking on the value of 1 in such years.

Source: Actual price data were obtained from the following sources supplemented by unpublished data from the U.S. Department of Agriculture: U.S. Department of Agriculture, *Agricultural Statistics*, U.S. Government Printing Office, Washington, D.C., 1976; Canadian Wheat Board, *Annual Report*, Winnipeg, various issues; Bureau of Agricultural Economics, *Wheat: Situation and Outlook*, Canberra, Australia, 1975; Statistical Office of the European Communities, *Yearbook of Agricultural Statistics*, Luxembourg, 1976.

Cross-price elasticities must also be accounted for in coarse grains as in wheat. Except for a small amount of rice fed in Thailand, rice is typically not used as a livestock feed. The cross elasticity of the price of coarse grains and the price of rice is thus taken to be zero. Wheat, however, cannot be treated this way. Wheat is used as a feed grain in many places. The percentages vary by time and place. In the period 1964/65–1968/69, the percentage was 0 to 4 percent in South Africa, Thailand, Japan, United States, and Argentina; 14 percent in the EEC; 35 percent in Australia, and 59 percent in Canada. Obviously, wheat is an

important feed grain, especially in Canada and the EEC. The cross-price elasticities between the price of wheat and price of coarse grains used by the USDA are
shown in Table 6.2. These shares along with cross-price elasticities indicate feed
wheat is most important in Canada and the EEC. Unlike the wheat and rice
models, two other related feed price cross elasticities are relevant: they are high-
protein feeds and roughage. The difficulty in determining a price and an elasticity for the nonmarketed roughage and the uncertainty as to whether high-protein
feeds are complements or substitutes suggests they may be omitted as demand
shifters without introducing significant bias.

TABLE 6.2

Coarse Grain Income and Price Elasticities

Country	Bjarnason Coarse Grain Price	USDA Coarse Grain Price	USDA Wheat Price	USDA Income
U	−.45	−.4	.1	.45
C	−.59	−.5	.15	.3
G	−.25	−.4	.05	0
A	—	−.1	0	0
F	−.25	−.4	0	.15
T[a]	—	−.5	0	.5
E[b]	−.65	−.55	.17	.56
J	−.93	−.7	0	.5

[a]Southeast Asia figures.

[b]Weighted average of EEC–6 and UK figures; weights are percent of coarse grain consumption represented.

Sources: Harold F. Bjarnason, "An Economic Analysis of 1980 International Trade in
Feed Grains," Ph.D. dissertation, Department of Economics, University of Wisconsin, Madison, Table IV.1, p. 143; Rojko, Urban, and Naive, World Demand Prospects for Grain in
1980 with Emphasis on Trade by the Less Developed Countries, Table 11, pp. 35–37.

SAMPLE FORECASTS OF THE COARSE GRAIN
TRADE MODEL

The interrelatedness of trade flows and supply prices in a model of wheat
trade distinguished by place of production has previously been demonstrated by
examining the effects of single demand and supply side shocks. Since the implications of that analysis hold for coarse grains, we will examine the accuracy of
predictions of endogenous variables for the two sample periods 1964/65–1965/66
and 1967/68–1968/69.

The model has been applied to the eight regions mentioned earlier. August/ July years were used for Canada and the EEC-9; July/June years were used for all other regions. Changes in production and stocks, hence supply, were treated as exogenous; this leaves the number of total possible endogenous variables as follows: 64 flows, 64 demand prices, and 8 supply prices. To reduce this number we assumed the United States imported only from Canada, Canada only from the United States, the EEC from all regions except Thailand, Japan from all regions, and all other regions were exporters only; this decreased the number of endogenous flows and prices to 22 for each category, and the 8 supply prices remained. There are 8 changes in the rest of the world's imports that were taken as given so in all we have 52 equations in 52 unknowns.

To obtain the elasticity parameters for the demand submatrix, Bjarnason's own price elasticities for coarse grains were used. An elasticity of substitution of –3.0 was assumed in all markets and import shares were taken from a representative year for the period 1968. The matrixes of direct and cross-price elasticities that resulted, along with assumed homogenous values for Australia and Thailand, are shown in Tables 6.3 and 6.4.

Table 6.5 presents actual and predicted flow and supply price changes for 1964/65-1965/66. The year 1965/66 was a transition year for the newly formed EEC; the six members were trying to move toward a single community indicator price for grains. However, this had not yet been achieved and a variety of prices for coarse grains existed throughout the community; as a result no attempt was made to quantify import levies for the EEC-9. For 1964/65 the EEC-9 did not export to Japan and since ROW imports are exogenous, this constrains the EEC predicted consumption to be equal to actual. For Japan, domestic supply price is ignored since the government acted to stabilize internal prices and the model constrains Japan to consume its entire production. To avoid the large trend consumption figure for Thailand, the exogenous demand shifter was taken to be the actual change in consumption, 23 percent. These factors make it necessary to ignore the five flows DTT through DJJ in evaluating the correctness of the results. Fourteen of 17 flows and 5 of 7 supply prices have the correct sign. The results reflect large supply changes in three regions; the United States experienced about a 16 percent rise, Argentina an 18 percent fall, Australia a 35 percent fall, and the EEC-9 a 3 percent fall. This explains the general rise in prices that were moderated by the U.S. supply rise. The fact that export prices did not rise in Australia and Argentina as much as predicted stems from their domestic consumption being smaller and exports larger than predicted. This could result from the trend consumption variable failing to explain livestock producers' changes in demand or from national grain marketing organizations' subsidization of exports. The actual price variables used are export prices, under the assumption that domestic export price movements follow domestic price movements; if this is not the case, domestic demand may be incorrectly predicted.

TABLE 6.3

Direct Price Elasticities of Demand

Consumer	Price Change							
	United States	Canada	Argentina	Australia	South Africa	Thailand	EEC-9	Japan
United States	-.454	-2.996	—	—	—	—	—	—
Canada	-2.855	-.745	—	—	—	—	—	—
Argentina	—	—	-.250	—	—	—	—	—
Australia	—	—	—	-.250	—	—	—	—
South Africa	—	—	—	—	-.250	—	—	—
Thailand	—	—	—	—	—	-.250	—	—
EEC-9	-2.790	-2.989	-2.902	-2.991	-2.976	—	-1.099	—
Japan	-2.500	-2.990	-2.939	-2.971	-2.828	-2.939	-2.946	-1.904

Source: Compiled by the authors.

TABLE 6.4

Cross Price Elasticities of Demand

Consumer	Price Change							
	United States	Canada	Argentina	Australia	South Africa	Thailand	EEC-9	Japan
United States	2.546	.004	0	0	0	0	0	0
Canada	.145	2.255	0	0	0	0	0	0
Argentina	0	0	0	0	0	0	0	0
Australia	0	0	0	0	0	0	0	0
South Africa	0	0	0	0	0	0	0	0
Thailand	0	0	0	0	0	0	0	0
EEC-9	.210	.011	.098	.009	.024	0	1.901	0
Japan	.500	.010	.061	.029	.172	.061	.054	1.096

Source: Compiled by the authors.

TABLE 6.5

Predicted and Actual Percentage Changes in Endogenous Variables, 1964/65—65/66

Trade Flows	Predicted	Actual
DDU	13.448	11.911
DCU	22.583	27.252
DEU	31.653	49.475
DJU	36.485	40.152
DCC	6.558	1.623
DUC	−2.577	−29.688
DEC	17.597	68.692
DJC	22.415	−2.913
DGG	9.822	−9.526
DEG	−46.902	−26.086
DJG	−41.797	−51.438
DAA	−23.278	−34.447
DEA	−74.374	.529
DJA	−68.351	−71.429
DFF	10.674	19.454
DEF	−16.180	−39.294
DJF	−4.800	−99.620
DTT	21.277	22.581
DJT	6.502	6.447
DEE	−3.986	−3.986
DJE	6.993	0.0
DJJ	2.227	2.227
Supply prices		
DSPU	−5.155	.01
DSPC	.186	4.707
DSPG	24.191	1.096
DSPA	35.164	7.392
DSPF	10.841	14.254
DSPT	2.892	−8.493
DSPE	6.921	17.287
DSPJ	−	−

Source: Actual price data were obtained from the following sources supplemented by unpublished data from the U.S. Department of Agriculture: U.S. Department of Agriculture, *Agricultural Statistics*, U.S. Government Printing Office, Washington, D.C., 1976; Canadian Wheat Board, *Annual Report*, Winnipeg, various issues; Bureau of Agricultural Economics, *Wheat: Situation and Outlook*, Canberra, Australia, 1975; Statistical Office of the European Communities, *Yearbook of Agricultural Statistics*, Luxembourg, 1976.

Table 6.6 compares the sum of the absolute differences of predicted trade flow levels and actual levels with that for a naive model whose predicted flows are taken to be equal to last year's flows. The ratio of the sums of absolute prediction errors is 3.5, which is quite good. However, much of the efficiency of the Coarse Grain Trade Model (CGTM) is due to its accurate prediction of the U.S. own consumption, which experienced a large increase in the period. If we use

TABLE 6.6

Comparison of Naive Model and Coarse Grain Trade Model for Predicting Trade Flow Levels for 1965/66 (thousand metric tons)

| Trade Flow | Actual | Predicted | |
		CGTM	Naive (1964/65)
DUU	129,799	131,581	115,984
DCU	551	530	433
DEU	13,807	12,161	9,237
DJU	4,433	4,317	3,163
DCC	11,523	11,620	10,905
DUC	180	249	256
DEC	722	503	428
DJC	200	252	206
DGG	4,027	4,888	4,451
DEG	3,167	2,274	4,282
DJG	152	182	313
DAA	1,629	1,907	2,485
DEA	380	97	378
DJA	52	58	182
JEF	4,728	4,380	3,958
DFF	258	356	425
DJF	1	250	263
DTT	38	38	31
DJT	776	776	729
DEE	42,703	42,703	44,476
DJE	0	0	0
DJJ	1,377	1,377	1,347

Source: Actual price data were obtained from the following sources supplemented by unpublished data from the U.S. Department of Agriculture: U.S. Department of Agriculture, *Agricultural Statistics*, U.S. Government Printing Office, Washington, D.C., 1976; Canadian Wheat Board, *Annual Report*, Winnipeg, various issues; Bureau of Agricultural Economics, *Wheat: Situation and Outlook*, Canberra, Australia, 1975; Statistical Office of the European Communities, *Yearbook of Agricultural Statistics*, Luxembourg, 1976.

TABLE 6.7

Predicted and Actual Percentage Changes in Endogenous Variables, 1967/68–1968/69

Trade Flows	Predicted	Actual
DUU	−1.223	3.990
DCU	11.276	.611
DEU	−25.166	−25.339
DJU	0.0	2.162
DCC	−2.424	−.066
DUC	−14.923	18.750
DEC	−41.721	−38.863
DJC	−12.355	−88.172
DGG	4.742	−7.258
DEG	13.888	11.862
DJG	50.886	828.571
DAA	12.929	−4.789
DEA	35.163	304.202
DJA	88.719	167.327
DFF	−.504	2.668
DEF	−22.127	−43.464
DJF	−2.681	8.580
DTT	96.111	74.286
DJT	−28.153	−25.806
DEE	−.113	−.871
DJE	54.293	626.471
DJJ	2.893	2.893
DSPU	6.593	−5.857
DSPC	11.160	−12.465
DSPG	−12.463	−5.245
DSPA	−27.157	−16.305
DSPF	8.714	−.454
DSPT	15.557	−7.211
DSPE	−	−
DSPJ	−	−

Source: Actual price data were obtained from the following sources supplemented by unpublished data from the U.S. Department of Agriculture: U.S. Department of Agriculture, *Agricultural Statistics*, U.S. Government Printing Office, Washington, D.C., 1976; Canadian Wheat Board, *Annual Report*, Winnipeg, various issues; Bureau of Agricultural Economics, *Wheat: Situation and Outlook*, Canberra, Australia, 1975; Statistical Office of the European Communities, *Yearbook of Agricultural Statistics*, Luxembourg, 1976.

the CGTM prediction for DUU in the naive model, the efficiency statistic would fall to 1.3, which, nevertheless, reflects a superior performance by the CGTM.

The predicted and actual flow and supply price changes for 1967/68–1968/69 are shown in Table 6.7. The transition of the EEC to a uniform indicator price in 1968/69 was essentially complete. In order to reflect the tariff on all imported grains, the average actual levies on barley, maize, oats, and sorghum were weighted by their imports and the percent change in these levies was used in the exogenous demand shift vector for EEC imports. Since EEC export subsidies were not quantified, DSPE is not reported. The assumptions made for Japan are the same as in the previous example. The trend consumption variable for Thailand was arbitrarily set to 1.0 for this run. Only the DJJ flow will not be considered in the evaluation. Fifteen of 21 flows but only 2 of 6 supply price predictions are in the correct direction. Since EEC supply fell only 2 percent in 1968/69, the inclusion of the variable levy was instrumental in the excellent prediction of EEC-9 reductions in imports. Large supply changes were an 11 percent rise in Argentina, a 16 percent rise in Australia, and an 8 percent decline in South Africa; domestic consumption in each of these countries was not predicted well with possible reasons being discussed earlier. The general slowdown in consumption growth rate together with large EEC levies and plentiful supplies were probably responsible for the lowered supply prices.

Table 6.8 examines levels of flows and presents a ratio of absolute prediction errors of 1.089. This is a decline in the efficiency of the CGTM from that in the 1965/66 example. The small increase in world consumption improved the naive model's performance.

The prediction for coarse grain flows and prices, as those for wheat, are superior to those of a naive forecast. Adding structure from economic theory improves the forecasting framework. We have not invested as much effort in incorporating policy shifters in the coarse grain market as we did for wheat in the 1973/74 forecasts. As a consequence we cannot say with much confidence how great an improvement one could expect in the forecasting capability from such an investment. Overall the limited evidence from the two experiments would indicate that the coarse grain model does as well as the wheat model. The accuracy could be improved, but that improvement must await further investment in information on exogenous variables.

RICE TRADE

Rice is a major food grain, but unlike wheat, hardly any is used as animal feed. While world production of rice is nearly as large in million tons units as wheat, the volume of trade is much less. Most rice is consumed in the area where it is produced. (See Tables 6.9, 6.10, and 6.11 for data on world production and trade in rice.) The United States is a major rice exporter, exporting more than

TABLE 6.8

Comparison of Naive Model and Coarse Grain Trade Model
for Predicting Trade Flow Levels for 1968/69
(thousand metric tons)

| Trade Flow | Actual | Predicted | |
		CGTM	Naive (1967/68)
DUU	137,399	130,511	132,127
DCU	824	911	819
DEU	6,983	6,999	9,353
DJU	4,490	4,395	4,395
DCC	12,025	11,741	12,033
DUC	190	136	160
DEC	258	246	422
DJC	58	408	465
DGG	5,418	6,119	5,842
DEG	3,376	3,437	3,018
DJA	910	148	98
DAA	22,147	2,547	2,255
DEA	481	161	119
DJA	270	191	101
DFF	5,195	5,034	5,060
DEF	839	1,156	1,484
DJF	1,506	1,350	1,387
DTT	122	137	70
DJT	483	468	651
DEE	50,849	51,238	51,296
DJE	494	105	68
DJJ	1,067	1,067	1,037

Source: Actual price data were obtained from the following sources supplemented by unpublished data from the U.S. Department of Agriculture: U.S. Department of Agriculture, *Agricultural Statistics*, U.S. Government Printing Office, Washington, D.C., 1976; Canadian Wheat Board, *Annual Report*, Winnipeg, various issues; Bureau of Agricultural Economics, *Wheat: Situation and Outlook*, Canberra, Australia, 1975; Statistical Office of the European Communities, *Yearbook of Agricultural Statistics*, Luxembourg, 1976.

half of its annual production. While rice is a relatively minor crop for the United States, its role in international trade has led us to do some initial modeling for it also.

Asian countries actively trade rice with other Asian countries. That area is also the largest importer of U.S. rice. Latin America and Africa represent areas of considerable rice production, but not much trade. The EEC-9 are importers

TABLE 6.9

Milled Rice Production
(thousand metric tons)

Year	World	Endog- enous	United States	EEC-9	Japan	East Asia	South- east Asia	South Asia	Exog- enous	People's Republic of China	Other
1964	181,829	103,628	2,386	520	11,451	17,667	18,027	53,577	78,201	60,846	17,355
1965	175,167	94,763	2,497	423	11,292	17,911	18,001	44,639	80,404	64,260	16,144
1966	178,260	95,677	2,805	503	11,598	18,821	18,367	43,583	82,583	65,559	17,024
1967	192,171	106,587	2,950	602	13,152	18,536	18,618	52,729	85,584	68,156	17,428
1968	195,254	112,391	3,459	503	13,148	20,896	18,619	55,766	82,863	64,899	17,964
1969	202,450	117,288	3,003	666	12,743	22,792	20,555	57,529	85,162	66,572	18,590
1970	210,153	117,562	2,796	633	11,547	23,947	20,471	58,168	92,591	72,529	20,062
1971	212,428	117,075	2,837	676	9,907	24,195	20,545	58,915	95,353	76,582	18,771
1972	204,447	110,082	2,828	561	10,819	23,297	18,662	53,915	94,365	74,392	19,973
1973	219,506	122,560	3,035	773	11,056	25,675	21,043	60,978	96,946	76,406	20,540
1974	223,295	120,483	3,667	728	11,186	27,040	21,123	56,739	102,812	81,600	21,212
1975	238,349	132,014	4,167	681	11,980	27,973	22,739	64,474	106,335	82,960	23,375
1976	241,080	131,858	3,600	697	11,610	28,481	22,910	64,560	109,222	85,000	24,222

Source: Working tables ERS, USDA.

TABLE 6.10

Major Importers of Milled Rice
(thousand metric tons)

	1964	1965	1966	1967	1968	1969	1970	1971	1972	1973	1974	1975	1976
EEC–9	427	411	483	464	438	476	438	512	524	595	579	510	523
Japan	410	880	893	475	298	52	15	10	–	24	57	36	5
East Asia	2,498	1,776	1,754	1,784	1,975	2,337	2,533	3,060	3,328	3,289	3,360	2,227	1,895
South Asia	1,612	1,621	1,621	1,569	1,168	1,012	831	1,238	653	438	653	1,005	1,105
Southeast Asia	83	169	465	788	711	398	623	219	487	491	305	430	380
Central Africa	516	550	514	447	508	533	660	748	705	715	680	565	386
Centrally Planned Economies	663	528	603	533	677	584	565	628	564	388	296	286	384
World	7,057	7,012	7,317	6,931	6,663	6,300	6,563	7,516	7,524	7,484	7,272	6,904	6,738

Source: Working tables ERS, USDA.

TABLE 6.11

Milled Rice Exports
(thousand metric tons)

	1964	1965	1966	1967	1968	1969	1970	1971	1972	1973	1974	1975	1976
United States	1,327	1,517	1,320	1,828	1,893	1,913	1,791	1,481	2,033	1,630	1,725	2,135	1,800
EEC–9	135	177	102	201	313	223	364	378	512	339	349	725	423
Japan	—	—	—	—	—	300	508	910	217	572	305	57	—
East Asia	311	438	386	232	275	132	69	100	209	138	80	71	45
Southeast Asia	3,929	3,647	2,806	2,341	1,615	1,484	1,879	2,369	2,814	1,093	1,245	1,207	1,750
South Asia	319	460	385	448	369	447	378	449	516	1,124	835	690	930
Subtotal	6,021	6,239	4,999	5,050	4,465	4,499	4,989	5,687	6,301	4,896	4,539	4,885	4,948
People's Republic of China	912	1,010	1,264	1,198	957	801	978	965	816	1,976	1,902	1,500	1,200
World	7,837	8,285	7,493	7,451	6,811	6,808	7,494	7,993	8,267	7,925	7,443	7,336	7,825
Endogenous as a percent of world	76.8	75.3	66.7	67.8	65.6	66.1	66.6	71.1	76.2	61.8	61.0	66.6	63.2

Source: Working tables ERS, USDA.

and are included in our endogenous regions. This institutional setting has several implications that distinguish the rice market from the wheat market. There are a larger number of exporting countries that should be considered endogenous, even though each of them is much smaller in terms of the quantity of rice shipped. Second, a larger portion of the rice trade is among developing countries. This latter fact presents no problems in principle, but it does have implications for data availability and reliability. Developing countries also at times interfere with the pricing mechanism in ways that are not as clearly specified as the policies we discuss for wheat. The main additional problem for rice is that more endogenous countries should be included so that regional aggregates become practical.

In particular, to describe a majority of rice exports and imports, the world would best be divided into six regions: United States, EEC-9, Japan, East Asia, Southeast Asia, and South Asia. The last three regions are ERS-USDA classifications. East Asia includes Indonesia, Hong Kong, Singapore, South Korea, Taiwan, Brunei, Macao, Philippines, Malaysia, Sabah, and Sarawak. Southeast Asia includes Thailand, Burma, Khmer, Laos, and South Vietnam. South Asia includes India, Afghanistan, Bangladesh, Bhutan, Nepal, Pakistan, and Sri Lanka. For 1965/75 those six regions accounted for 68 percent of world rice exports and 67 percent of world rice imports.

PREDICTION OF HISTORICAL TRADE FLOWS

For years in which sufficient data were available we used the simple Armington-type model to predict historical trade flows and prices for rice. As for wheat and feed grains, output was taken to be fixed, and inventory levels to be unchanged so the model contained supply shifters rather than supply equations. Supply prices were endogenous, however, so that given output changes were allowed to affect all prices. That is, actual percentage changes in rice output for the six endogenous regions for selected years were introduced as exogenous shifters. The model was solved for the resulting percentage changes in trade flows (domestic disappearance and international trade), consumer prices, and supply prices. In this initial stage, no price shifters were introduced so that supply and consumer prices changed together.

Tables 6.12 and 6.13 show export and import trade shares based on calendar-year data for 1964, 1969, and 1970. These trade shares were used in applying the model to predict trade flow and price changes for 1964/65, 1965/66, 1969/70, and 1970/71.* As shown in another section, export shares are used in

---

*Since the trade share matrixes for 1969 and 1970 are almost identical, calculations for 1969/70 and 1970/71 were based on the 1969 trade share matrixes.

TABLE 6.12

Export Shares

Producer	Consumer						
	United States	EEC	Japan	East Asia	Southeast Asia	South Asia	Rest of World
				1964			
United States	.405	.045	.048	.081	.000	.123	.298
EEC	0	.825	0	0	0	0	.175
Japan	0	0	1	0	0	0	0
East Asia	.001	0	.007	.989	0	.000	.003
Southeast Asia	0	.006	.009	.111	.788	.039	.047
South Asia	0	0	0	.000	0	.998	.002
Rest of world	00	.005	.001	.021	0	.012	.961
				1969			
United States	..409	.063	.001	.242	0	.139	.146
EEC	.001	.628	0	.078	0	0	.293
Japan	0	0	.968	.030	0	.002	.000
East Asia	0	0	0	.998	0	0	.002
Southeast Asia	0	.001	.003	.030	.942	.008	.016
South Asia	0	.002	0	0	0	.998	.0008
Rest of world	.000	.003	.000	.008	.005	.005	.979
				1970			
United States	.399	.057	.000	.225	0	.174	.145
EEC	.031	.362	0	.199	0	0	.409
Japan	0	0	.943	.044	0	.010	.003
East Asia	0	0	0	.999	0	.000	.001
Southeast Asia	0	.001	.002	.030	.947	.003	.017
South Asia	0	.000	0	.000	0	.998	.002
Rest of world	.000	.004	0	.008	.007	.002	.979

Source: Compiled by the authors from working tables ERS, USDA.

TABLE 6.13

Import Shares

	Consumer						
Producer	United States	EEC	Japan	East Asia	Southeast Asia	South Asia	Rest of World
			1964				
United States	.990	.136	.009	.009	0	.005	.030
EEC	0	.569	.0	0	0	0	.004
Japan	0	0	.965	0	0	0	0
East Asia	.010	0	.010	.860	0	0	.003
Southeast Asia	0	.161	.014	.107	1	.014	.040
South Asia	0	0	0	.000	0	.976	.004
Rest of world	0	.134	.002	.024	0	.005	.919
			1969				
United States	.999	.279	.000	.033	0	.008	.006
EEC	0005	.354	0	.001	0	0	.001
Japan	0	0	.995	.014	0	.001	.000
East Asia	0	0	0	.903	0	0	.005
Southeast Asia	0	.026	.005	.022	.976	.002	.003
South Asia	0	.004	0	0	0	.982	.001
Rest of world	.0005	.337	.000	.027	.024	.007	.988
			1970				
United States	.983	.240	.000	.027	0	.009	.005
EEC	.014	.278	0	.004	0	0	.003
Japan	0	0	.997	.018	0	.002	.000
East Asia	0	0	0	.903	0	.000	.000
Southeast Asia	0	.040	.003	.023	.968	.001	.004
South Asia	0	.012	0	.000	0	.986	.002
Rest of world	.003	.430	0	.025	.032	.002	.986

Source: Compiled by the authors from working tables ERS, USDA.

the equilibrium condition, and the import shares are used to calculate the demand price elasticities. Those elasticities are shown in Table 6.14. In addition to the import shares, they are based on the assumption that $\sigma = -3$ and the basic demand elasticities are $-.2$ for the United States, $-.1$ for Southeast Asia, and $-.3$ for the EEC, Japan, and South Asia. These are the η estimates reported by Rojko.

The solutions to the model for the four selected years are given in Table 6.15. The exogenous output changes are given by the DI in the table. Other exogenous shifters were trend terms and transport cost changes. Because of data availability it was assumed that the percentage change in rice and wheat transport costs were equal. Trend terms were taken from Rojko et al. (1971).

The percentage changes in each region's total exports and the price changes are consistent with the exogenous shifters. The table shows, however, that prediction of percentage changes in country-to-country trade flows and prices is generally not very accurate when comparing actual and predicted changes. The only flow changes generally predicted accurately are the own trade flow changes for regions that consume most of their output.

We might expect the rice model to be more sensitive to errors in σ than the wheat model since all endogenous regions in the rice model both export and import rice. In this case more flows depend on the elasticity of substitution than in the case of wheat where only one region is both an exporter and importer. When we changed σ to -10, however, the predicted endogenous variables did not change significantly.

Since we included no government policy changes, the inaccuracy in exogenous shifters may be a major source of the errors. For example, EEC import duties were among the policies not included as exogenous shifters. As for the EEC in the wheat model, care must be taken in modeling flows and prices for EEC, East Asia, Southeast Asia, and South Asia. Modeling EEC behavior for rice is no different than for wheat. A combination of levies and export subsidies are used to accommodate the Common Agricultural Policy for rice. The levy is the difference between the threshold price and the lowest c.i.f. import price. Threshold prices vary by type of rice and are determined by the Duisberg quotations on Italian rice varieties (USDA 1970). Precisely predicting the levy, then, poses the same kind of problem as was discussed for wheat. As noted, the use of yearly averages may minimize the empirical relevance of such a problem.

Because the Asian regional aggregates account for a majority of trade, it is likely that inaccurate data for the endogenous variables is also a factor in our poor forecasts. These regions do not have common agricultural or monetary policies. This makes accurate prediction of differences between producer prices and import prices more difficult since the appropriate prices are functions of exchange rates and policy variables among the countries within the regions. There are actually two problems raised here: (1) the above-mentioned quantification of exogenous shocks becomes more difficult and (2) prediction accuracy

TABLE 6.14

Price Elasticities

Price change	Consumer					
	United States	EEC	Japan	East Asia	Southeast Asia	South Asia
	Direct Price					
	(based on 1964 trade shares)					
United States	−.228	−2.633	−2.976	−2.976	−	−2.987
EEC	−	−1.464	−	−	−	−
Japan	−	−	−.395	−	−	−
East Asia	−2.972	−	−2.973	−.678	−	−
Southeast Asia	−	−2.565	−2.962	−2.711	−.1	−2.962
South Asia	−	−	−	−	−	−.365
	Direct Price					
	(based on 1969 trade shares)					
United States	−.203	−2.247	−	−2.911	−	−2.978
EEC	−2.999	−2.0442	−	−2.997	−	−
Japan	−	−	−.314	−2.962	−	−2.997
East Asia	−	−	−	−.562	−	−
Southeast Asia	−	−2.930	−2.987	−2.941	−.170	−2.995
South Asia	−	−2.989	−	−	−	−.349
	Cross price					
	(based on 1964 trade shares)					
United States	2.772	.367	.024	.024	−	.014
EEC	−	1.536	−	−	−	−
Japan	−	−	2.606	−	−	−
East Asia	.028	−	.027	2.322	−	−
Southeast Asia	−	.435	.038	.289	−.170	.038
South Asia	−	−	−	−	−	2.635
	Cross Price					
	(based on 1969 trade shares)					
United States	2.797	.753	−	.089	−	.022
EEC	.0014	.956	−	.003	−	−
Japan	−	−	2.687	.038	−	.003
East Asia	−	−	−	2.438	−	−
Southeast Asia	−	.070	+.014	.059	2.830	.005
South Asia	−	.011	−	−	−	2.651
Rest of world	.0014	.910	−	.073	.070	−

Source: Compiled by the authors.

TABLE 6.15

Predicted and Actual Percentage Changes in Rice Flows and Supply Prices

	1964–55		1965–66		1969–70		1970–71	
	Actual	Predicted	Actual	Predicted	Actual	Predicted	Actual	Predicted
DUU	7.4	3.4	9.9	-.1	-10.1	5.4	3.2	1.5
DEU	6.4	50.4	51.3	24.3	-17.1	31.6	-20.0	.5
DJU	100.8	58.3	-64.2	-3.2	–	–	–	–
DIU	-90.6	9.7	18.6	-24.6	-14.7	-19.4	10.9	-18.5
DSU	38.1	47.1	1.8	.8	15.8	-44.0	-72.0	-44.7
DUE	–	–	–	–	195.8	-18.8	144.0	21.6
DEE	-28.3	-24.2	-24.3	-26.0	-24.5	15.7	51.3	19.9
DJE	–	–	–	–	231.9	-39.9	-87.6	-8.5
DJJ	-3.7	-3.7	-1.3	-1.3	-6.1	-4.0	11.6	9.7
DIJ	–	–	–	–	40.4	-30.6	49.2	146.8
DSJ	–	–	–	–	559.3	-55.3	61.7	120.2
DUI	-100.0	-4.4	0.0	26.4	–	–	–	–
DJI	-83.8	52.7	110.2	25.3	–	–	–	–
DII	.6	4.7	4.6	4.5	8.6	8.6	.6	.6
DET	-85.4	39.7	20.6	36.1	49.4	424.8	82.2	270.8
DJT	-.7	48.8	-43.3	9.6	-41.0	400.2	-2.6	114.9
DIT	-72.1	.2	-24.2	-11.7	14.4	375.5	4.3	252.9
DTT	1.7	1.5	3.5	.3	14.7	-2.2	-2.4	-12.3
DST	-42.0	37.5	-23.1	13.6	-61.1	350.8	126.3	226.2
DES	–	–	–	–	71.9	72.4	-22.1	39.5
DSS	3.5	3.8	-17.5	-17.6	5.0	4.4	-1.8	-1.7
SPU*	1.8	-16.1	1.8	1.8	7.4	-30.9	1.7	-10.9
SPE	NA	8.7	NA	16.2	NA	-24.3	NA	-17.3
SPJ	9.1	4.8	9.4	-1.1	.3	-26.4	5.7	-67.4
SPI	30.4	-14.4	.2	-10.2	35.3	-38.8	-5.6	-18.4
SPT	13.3	-13.2	+41.6	-5.1	-5.0	-163.5	-15.3	-103.8
SPS	-10.1	-13.6	+29.5	46.4	-11.1	-45.6	.4	-26.4

*U, E, J, I, T, and S stand for United States, EEC-9, Japan, East Asia, Southeast Asia, and South Asia.

Source: Actual price data were obtained from the following sources supplemented by unpublished data from the U.S. Department of Agriculture: U.S. Department of Agriculture, *Agricultural Statistics*, U.S. Government Printing Office, Washington, D.C., 1976; Canadian Wheat Board, *Annual Report*, Winnipeg, various issues; Bureau of Agricultural Economics, *Wheat: Situation and Outlook*, Canberra, Australia, 1975; Statistical Office of the European Communities, *Yearbook of Agricultural Statistics*, Luxembourg, 1976.

is difficult to determine because the relevant price for comparison is ambiguous. Given adequate data, however, it would be possible to construct effective exchange rates and composite supply of import prices for the aggregate regions. Unfortunately, if price and policy data for all of the countries in those aggregates are not available, then prices in the major countries must be used. This practice increases the potential margin of error. That these regions are developing countries also raises doubt as to the quality of data available for modeling their trade.

REFERENCES

Australia, Bureau of Agricultural Economics. *The Coarse Grain Situation*. Canberra.

Bjarnason, Harold F. 1967. "An Economic Analysis of 1980 International Trade in Feed Grains." Ph.D. dissertation, Department of Economics, University of Wisconsin, Madison.

Canada Crops Section. *Grain Trade of Canada*. Ohawa.

Commonwealth Economic Committee. 1971. *Grain Crops*. London.

Commonwealth Secretariat. *Grain Crops: A Review*. London.

———. *Rice Bulletin*. London.

Food and Agriculture Organization of the United Nations. *Monthly Bulletin of Agricultural and Economic Statistics*. Rome.

———. *National Grain Policies*. Rome.

———. *Production Yearbook*. Rome.

———. *Rice Report*. Rome.

———. Trade Yearbook. *Rome.*

———. *World Grain Trade Statistics*. Rome.

Hildreth, Clifford and F. G. Jarrett. 1955. *A Statistical Study of Livestock Production and Marketing*. Cowles Commission Monograph 15. New York: Wiley.

International Monetary Fund. 1971. *International Financial Statistics*. Washington, D.C.

International Wheat Council. 1974. *World Wheat Statistics*. London.

Moore, John R., Sammy Elaassar, and Billy Lessley. 1971. *Least Cost World Trade Patterns for Grains and Meats*. College Park: University of Maryland, Department of Agricultural and National Resources.

Organization for Economic Cooperation and Development. *Statistics of Foreign Trade*. Series C, Paris.

Rojko, Anthony, Francis Urban, and James Naive. 1971. *World Demand Prospects for Grain in 1980 with Emphasis on Trade by the Less Developed Countries*. Washington, D.C.: U.S. Department of Agriculture.

United Nations. *Commodity Trade Statistics*. Statistical Office of the United Nations. New York.

U.S. Department of Agriculture. *Foreign Agriculture Circular*, Foreign Agricultural Service, Washington, D.C.: U.S. Government Printing Office.

——. *Rice Situation*. Washington, D.C.: U.S. Government Printing Office.

——. 1968. *World Trade in Selected Agricultural Commodities: 1951-65*. Foreign Agricultural Economic Report No. 45. Economic Research Service. Washington, D.C.: U.S. Government Printing Office.

——. 1970. *The Grain Price System of the European Community*. FAS M–224, Foreign Agricultural Service, Washington, D.C.: U.S. Government Printing Office.

——. 1976a. "Rice Production and Trade for Major Regions, Countries, and the World." Washington, D.C.: Foreign Agricultural Service, mimeographed.

——. 1976b. "Data Book: World Rice Study." Agricultural Experiment Stations of Arkansas and Texas, mimeographed.

7

FOREIGN TRADE CONTROLS, DEVALUATION, AND DOMESTIC GRAIN PRICES, 1973-74

The crop year 1973-74 was a turbulent one for the world grain market. The large decrease in world grain production of the previous year had been partly met by inventory decumulation in North America. These net sales from inventories attenuated the price increase in 1972-73, but it left the world more vulnerable to disturbances in the grain market in the following year. In spite of a record world wheat crop and a sharp decline in Soviet wheat imports, wheat prices doubled in 1973-74 to the highest level since 1947. Many explanations for this large and rapid price increase have been offered, and we will try to evaluate the relative importance of several of them in terms of our world trade model.

Because of its prominence in the economic literature, we demonstrate how to measure the effect of currency markets on wheat prices in the United States (Schuh 1974). Specifically we ask how much of the observed increase in wheat prices could be attributed to devaluation of the dollar. This issue arose earlier in connection with the 1933 dollar devaluation when one of the advance justifications offered was that it would increase prices of agricultural products (Friedman and Schwartz 1963, pp. 465-66). Several empirical studies of the 1933 episode have been done (Davis 1935; Timoshenko 1938), and they appear to conclude that the devaluation had a negligible effect on U.S. wheat prices.

ECONOMIC POLICY IN 1973-74

Fluctuation in production and inventories was accompanied by major policy changes in both exporting and importing countries as they sought to insulate themselves from the price changes in the international wheat market.

106

The most important policy changes occurred in endogenous countries outside the United States, and these changes can be entered as exogenous shifters in our price equations. Changes in the exogenous shifters were shown earlier in Table 5.8, and the column pertaining to 1973-74 is repeated here in Table 7.1. This table also shows the multipliers from row 27 for the U.S. supply price for the same year.*

If one looked only at the three exogenous shifters that have the largest impact on the U.S. price—the demand shifter, the change in supply, and the change in exogenous exports—the predicted increase in the U.S. price would be 8.28 percent. The 6.1 percent change from increased maize price, and income change and the 3.67 percent decrease in supply, give a positive impetus to the price, while the decreased exports give a negative one. Since we know that the U.S. price rose substantially more than this, we obviously need to include a great deal more information about the world in a model to forecast prices.

Our plan in this chapter is to review some of the major policy changes that were made by governments in the 1973-74 year. We then trace through the wheat model the impact of these changes and compare them to certain other changes. One of the variables that has been alleged to have had a significant impact on prices in this particular year is the devaluation of the dollar. We give special attention to this variable.

European Community Actions

The EEC applies a variable levy to wheat imports and automatically insulates the domestic price from changes in foreign prices. In 1972-74 world prices, although high by historical standards, were low relative to the EEC threshold price, and the levy averaged $50 per ton. In 1973-74 world prices continued to rise and the levy fell to zero for most of the year. This encouragement to imports was supplemented by banning exports to certain regions of the world and taxing exports to other regions.

---

*One thing to keep in mind when interpreting the forecasts is that supply is exogenous. While we show both an endogenous demand price and an endogenous supply price, they are really the same for the six endogenous own prices. That is, the SPU forecast (supply price change, U.S.) simply repeats the DPUU forecast (demand price change, U.S.). This forecast is really the change at the wholesale level, say, of the country in question. Most of the regions involved pursue, or have pursued, domestic subsidy programs to their producers. Thus there are wedges driven between the producer and consumer prices that we have not attempted to capture. These comments are especially relevant for Canada and Australia where the "true" producer price is sometimes not known until long after harvest.

TABLE 7.1

Exogenous Shifters and Multipliers for
U.S. Internal Price, 1973–74

	Shifter	Multiplier (row 27)
Change in demand		
UU	6.1	1.51
EU	6.0	.19
JU	.9	.23
CC	11.3	.13
EC	6.0	.08
JC	.9	.05
AA	1.4	.61
EA	6.0	0
JA	.9	.08
GG	4.2	.08
EG	6.0	.01
EE	6.0	.85
JJ	.9	.05
Price difference		
UU	–	.69
EU	–10.2	–.51
JU	–38.3	–.18
CC	–	–.03
EC	24.6	–.05
JC	12.7	.07
AA	–	–.06
EA	41.8	.10
JA	29.0	–.04
GG	–	–.02
EG	–8.5	.02
EE	–	0
JJ	–	0
Change in supply		
U	–3.7	–3.78
C	–25.0	–.46
A	36.5	–2.04
G	–61.3	–.10
E	–10.4	–.95
J	–33.7	–.05
Exogenous exports to ROW		
U	–8.0	1.85
C	–40.8	.20
A	72.6	1.35
G	–76.7	.02
E	–33.0	.10

Source: Compiled by the authors.

Japanese Actions

Japan engages in state trading. The Food Agency is the monopoly importer for wheat. Prior to 1973 the agency bought wheat at the world price and sold to Japanese millers at a higher price, the difference constituting an effective tariff. In 1973–74 the agency insulated Japanese consumers from the increase in world prices by selling domestically at a loss. The subsidy amounted to a 57 percent decrease in the internal price from 1972–73. They continued this import subsidy until it was phased out in early 1976.

Canadian and Australian Actions

After the United States, Canada and Australia are the most important wheat exporters. They both employ state trading agencies in the foreign sales of their wheat. In 1973–74 both agencies levied effective export taxes by selling to domestic millers at far below the export price. The Canadian Wheat Board's average export price was C$6.00 per bushel, while the price to domestic millers was C$3.25. This represents a 41 percent export tax. The Australian Wheat Board's export price was 53 percent higher than its domestic price.

Dollar Devaluation

Accurate estimation of the degree of overvaluation of a currency is difficult. When rates were fixed in the 1960s, Floyd estimated the overvaluation of the dollar at 10 percent (Floyd 1965a). When the dollar was allowed to float in 1971, the dollar depreciated by approximately 10 percent, thus verifying to a large extent the Floyd estimate.* In early 1973 the dollar was devalued again by an average of 10 percent, but there was a partial reversal by the end of the year.

Shipping Costs

The U.S. government has pursued several policies that have raised shipping costs paid by exporters of U.S. wheat (see Bennathan and Walters 1969 and Jantscher 1975).† These have included the promotion of shipping cartels or con-

---

*This depreciation is taken from the Economic Report of the President 1974, page 222. It is measured by the Morgan Guaranty trade weighted index.

†U.S. shipping policy is also held responsible for raising ocean freight rates by the Presidential Task Group on Antitrust Immunities in its January 1977 report.

ferences that collude to set monopoly freight rates and cargo preference laws that require exporters to use higher-cost U.S. ships when cheaper transport is available. An increase in shipping cost lowers the price received by U.S. sellers relative to the price paid by foreign importers. In this respect it acts like an export tax or a currency revaluation. The ongoing high-cost shipping policy depressed the U.S. wheat price in the same way as the overvalued dollar did prior to the 1971 devaluation. Shipping policy did not change in 1973–74, but retaining the historical policy depressed wheat prices relative to what they otherwise would have been. We can measure this shipping policy effect to determine whether it depressed wheat prices more than devaluation raised them.

In order to calculate the net impact of increased shipping costs, one needs to know what fraction of those costs are attributable to government policy. Reliable estimates of this effect are not readily available, but one study for the Federal Maritime Commission has attempted to measure the effect (Bennathan and Walters 1969). They observed that freight rates for U.S. exports exceeded those for U.S. imports by 32 percent, and they attributed this differential to the cartel.*

MEASURING THE IMPACT OF POLICIES

Before turning to the actual data for 1973–74 and analysis of government policy, let us review the mechanics of the model that allow us to separate effects of individual shifters. Recall that the model in its final use is deterministic and can be written as $XY = A$, and the solution for the endogenous variable can be written as $Y = X^{-1}A$. A particular endogenous variable can then be found from the appropriate row in X^{-1} and information on the exogenous variables in A. One variable of primary interest is the internal price of U.S. wheat. The multipliers for this variable are those shown in Table 7.1. Individual shocks such as the effect on the U.S. price of imposing a tariff on one particular kind of wheat by one country would be found from one element of the multiplier row and the percentage change in the tariff. A tariff on all wheat in the absence of any other changes would affect the price of U.S. wheat by an amount found from adding several elements of the multiplier row times the tarriff changes.

With this framework we have traced out the projected impacts of several changes that can be predicted with the model set up to forecast 1973–74 flows

---

*The shipping portion of the current five-year U.S.–USSR grain agreement also has the effect of depressing the U.S. price. The agreement specifies a range of exports and a negotiable price with the condition that a certain fraction be carried in high-cost U.S. ships. The shipping condition lowers the Soviet demand at a given price which reduced export volume and price.

and prices. These implications of the model have been collected in Table 7.2, where the percentage effect on the U.S. internal wheat price from various exogenous changes are shown. As an example consider the effect of a devaluation. There are two endogenous importers in the model, Europe and Japan. The devaluation enters as a shifter in the equations that relate the U.S. price in those countries to the U.S. supply price. The multipliers for those changes are -.51 for Europe and -.18 for Japan from Table 7.1. The 10 percent change in the dollar would have a 6.9 percent (5.1 + 1.8) change on the U.S. price when both markets are considered simultaneously. The other examples are calculated in this same straightforward manner. Let us now turn to the incorporation of the policy changes.

TABLE 7.2

Effect on the Price of Wheat in the United States of Certain Exogenous Changes

	DPUU (percent)
1. Decrease of EEC tariff by 10 percent on wheat from:	
United States	+2.5
Canada	+.1
Argentina	-.2
All imports	+2.4
2a. Increase in Canadian export tax by 10 percent on wheat sent to:	
Japan	+.3
Europe	-.1
All markets	+.2
2b. Increase in Australian export tax by 10 percent on wheat sent to:	
Japan	+.2
2c. Decrease in Japanese tariff by 10 percent on wheat from:	
United States	+.7
Canada	-.2
Australia	-.1
All imports	+.4
2a + 2b + 2c	+.8
3. U.S. devalue by 10 percent against:	
Europe	+5.1
Japan	+1.8
All currencies	+6.9
4. Increase of 10 percent in cost of shipping U.S. wheat to:	
Europe	-0.9
Japan	-0.6
All markets	-1.5

Source: Compiled by the authors.

TABLE 7.3

Actual and Forecast Rates of Change in Real Wheat Prices, 1972-73 to 1973-74, for Different Wheat Policies

Variable	Actual Change	1972-73 Policies	1972-73 Plus EEC Variable Levy Change	1973-74 Policies
Internal prices[a]				
United States	59.1	30.3	39.7	51.2
Canada	15.7	30.9	43.5	12.3
Australia	-9.0	7.6	19.0	-24.5
Argentina	b	126.8	135.4	137.0
Europe	0	37.0	32.0	35.8
Japan	5.4	50.7	59.9	25.1

[a]The actual prices are internal wholesale price changes. The forecast prices are internal consumption price changes for the country's own wheat.

[b]Argentina embargoed wheat exports in early 1973-74 and controlled prices so rigidly that quoted prices are virtually meaningless.

Source: Actual price data were obtained from the following sources supplemented by unpublished data from the U.S. Department of Agriculture: U.S. Department of Agriculture, *Agricultural Statistics*, U.S. Government Printing Office, Washington, D.C., 1976; Canadian Wheat Board, *Annual Report*, Winnipeg, various issues; Bureau of Agricultural Economics, *Wheat: Situation and Outlook*, Canberra, Australia, 1975; Statistical Office of the European Communities, *Yearbook of Agricultural Statistics*, Luxembourg, 1976.

The basic data for the analysis of policy changes is contained in Table 7.3, which repeats for emphasis some of the internal price information from Table 5.8. The second column shows the actual internal percentage price change for each country listed from 1972-73 to 1973-74. The next column shows the price change forecast if the 1972-73 policy regimes had been followed by the governments of the countries involved. The important thing to notice is that in the absence of policy changes, but in the presence of other shifters, the U.S. price is forecast to increase less, but all other prices are forecast to be larger than actual. The shifters were a decrease in available supply, an increase in other grain prices, a net decrease in exogenous exports, and an increase in shipping costs.

The fourth column shows the forecast prices changes if all countries pursued their 1972-73 policies except for the EEC, which lowered its import levy by the amount it actually did in 1973-74. This shifts demand onto foreign wheat and it raises all wheat prices except the European one. The U.S. price forecast rises from 30.3 percent to 39.7 percent. Finally we introduce the actual 1973–74 trade policies of Canada, Australia, and Japan, which we de-scribed above. When all of these insulating trade policies are incorporated simul-taneously, the results can be seen in the final column. The marginal effect is to shift demand onto U.S. wheat and to increase the forecast of the U.S. wheat price to 51.2 percent, which is a further improvement. The Canadian price fore-cast is much smaller and closer to the actual, the Australian price is now cor-rectly forecast to decrease, and the Japanese price forecast is for a smaller in-crease, which is closer to the actual.

We conclude that government policy in the major wheat-trading countries was responsible for much of the large price increase in the United States in 1973–74. We did not include a devaluation adjustment in the immediately pre-ceding calculation.* As shown earlier in Table 7.2, however, a 10 percent de-valuation against both Europe and Japan would have explained only another 7 percent of the nearly 60 percent U.S. price increase. Despite the attention that has been given to devaluation as a cause of price increases in 1973–74 (Schuh 1974), our calculations imply that devaluation was less important in this episode than government trade policies. In addition one can estimate the relative im-portance of shipping policy for U.S. wheat prices. The 30 percent increase in shipping costs mentioned above would have depressed the U.S. domestic price by 4 to 5 percent.†

OVERVALUATION AND FACTOR PRICES IN AGRICULTURE

The impact of the policies discussed above is not confined to the price of the product involved. Product prices affect factor prices if factors are specific to the industry. Agricultural land is an obvious example of such a factor and specialized labor may be a quasi-fixed factor. Lopes and Schuh (1976), in a sequel to the basic Schuh reference, look at this distributional aspect of inter-national trade distortions and product price changes. They point out that a

---

*The main reason for not including an actual devaluation in our calculations is the difficulty of specifying the correct size. In the winter of 1973 the dollar was allowed to float. A clear devaluation of the dollar against certain currencies resulted. The crop year 1973–74 does not begin until July 1, 1973. During the course of the crop year currencies re-aligned from the initial changes in early calendar 1973. The maximum devaluation against any currency would be the 10 percent used for illustration. The real devaluation for U.S. wheat customers was substantially less.

† This figure can be obtained by adjusting the figure in Table 7.2 for a 30 percent cost increase. The multipliers for row 27 from Table 7.1 (–.51 and –.18) times the change in shipping costs weighted by their fraction of the U.S. export price (.18 and .34) yield the figures in Table 7.2.

persistent overvaluation of the dollar, absent any other changes, has the effect of lowering product prices and thus land rents. This has the opposite effect on factor rewards to land from the usual array of income support measures for agriculture.

Floyd (1965b) has constructed a six-equation model of the agricultural sector, which provides links between product and factor prices. He provides numerical estimates of the parameters of the system so that for specified policies affecting agricultural output one can put limits on the resulting changes in output price, factor use, and factor prices. Lopes and Schuh use this framework for their qualitative analysis. It should be instructive, then, to carry the analysis further by using the numbers adduced in the first part of the paper to calculate some impacts on factor rewards. Specifically the relative size of the impact of overvaluation and trade controls on factor prices is measured.

How important were monetary forces in altering agricultural land values in 1973-74? This is a complex question since land has many alternative uses and our model concentrates on wheat. However, we might gain some insights into the relationship by noting that most product prices (food grains, feed grains, soybeans, cotton) tended to move together during this period, so the wheat price might serve as a crude index of all other prices.

Floyd's model implies that factor prices will rise relative to product prices, the specific limits for the factor price change being 1.5 to 3 times the product price change. Our model predicts that a 10 percent devaluation will increase wheat prices by 7 percent. Thus the implied increase in land rent resulting from a 10 percent devluation would be 10.5 to 21 percent. Is there any evidence that land markets reflected changes of this magnitude?

Table 7.4 contains land price data for the period 1970-75 for real land price (reported values deflated by the Consumer Price Index [CPI]), the index of prices received for agricultural products, the ratio of prices received to the index of prices paid, and the CPI. Comparing the land price change in each year with the preceding year's product price change, it can be seen that in no year was the land price change as large as the product price change. A devaluation occurred in 1971 and product prices rose 7 percent in real terms while land values increased 4.5 percent. In the year 1973-74 there was a devaluation just prior to the beginning of the U.S. crop year. The real price of farm products rose by 19 percent from the calculations in Table 7.4 while the land price rose by 13.1 percent. For this year, then, land prices rose less than the all-product index, less than observed wheat prices, and less than our forecast wheat prices. These crude data do not seem consistent with the view that devaluation had a major effect on land markets.

The above evidence may not be a refutation of Floyd's model, since there are a number of identification problems associated with the table that were not considered. Since land is a durable asset, it should be important to distinguish

TABLE 7.4

Real Land Price Per Acre of U.S. Farmland and Prices
Received, 1970-75

	Real Land Price per Acre ($/acre)	Percent Change	Index of Prices Received	Price Ratio* (1967 = 100)	Consumer Price Index
1970	167.7		110	96	
1971	167.3	-.3	112	93	121.3
1972	174.8	4.5	126	100	125.3
1973	185.6	6.2	172	119	133.1
1974	209.9	13.1	184	109	147.7
1975	219.6	4.6	186	103	161.2

*Index of prices received divided by index of prices paid.

Sources: Farm Real Estate Market Developments, July 1976; *Agricultural Statistics*, 1975; and *Farm Index*, October 1976; U.S. Department of Agriculture: Washington, D.C.: Government Printing Office.

between transitory and permanent changes in land rent. The price of land is the present value of future expected land rent, and an event that raises present rent but not future rent will cause only a small increase in the land price. A possible explanation is that the variables that raised grain prices were perceived as transitory, and these perceptions have been vindicated by subsequent experience. All of the policies held responsible for raising prices in 1973-74 have subsequently been reversed. Japan has returned to its previous tariff policy, and the EEC has a higher wheat tariff in 1977 than it had in 1972. Canada, Australia, and Argentina are now promoting wheat exports instead of restricting them as they did in 1973-74. Although the dollar has moved unevenly against other currencies, on the average the 1973-74 devaluation has been more than reversed, since the dollar is worth 5 percent more in May 1977 than it was in February 1973 in terms of the Morgan Guaranty index. These transitory changes should not be expected to have a large impact on land prices.

The relationship between devaluation and land prices deserves more systematic study than we have provided. However, our interpretation of the data is that land prices rose less than product prices, and much of the observed product price increase seems attributable to government policies other than devaluation. Since this does not leave much of a residual to be explained by dollar devaluation, our tentative conclusion is that devaluation was probably not the dominant factor in the agricultural land market in 1973-74.

CONCLUSION

We have employed our model to analyze the behavior of the world wheat market in the volatile year of 1973-74. Several types of government policies were incorporated into the model, and their relative importance in affecting wheat prices, trade flows, and land values was assessed. Government trade policies designed to insulate domestic prices from foreign conditions were found to be the most important explanatory variable. Dollar devaluation made a smaller contribution to the price increase, and the high-cost shipping policy depressed the U.S. domestic wheat price.

REFERENCES

Bennathan, E. and A. A. Walters. 1969. *The Economics of Ocean Freight Rates*. New York: Praeger.

Davis, Joseph. 1935. *Wheat and the AAA*. Washington, D.C.: Brookings Institution.

Floyd, John. 1965a. "The Overvaluation of the Dollar." *American Economic Review* 55 (March): 95-107.

——. 1965b. "The Effects of Farm Price Supports on the Returns to Land and Labor in Agriculture." *Journal of Political Economy* 73 (April): 148-58.

Friedman, Milton and Anna Jacobson Schwartz. 1963. *A Monetary History of the United States: 1867-1960*. Princeton, N.J.: Princeton University Press.

Jantscher, Gerald R. 1975. *Bread Upon the Waters: Federal Aids to the Maritime Industries*. Washington, D.C.: Brookings Institution.

Lopes, Mauro and G. Edward Schuh. 1976. "Price Supports Versus an Equilibrium Exchange Rate: A Comparison of Income Distribution Consequences." Paper contributed to the annual meetings of the American Agricultural Economics Association, Pennsylvania State University, August.

Schuh, G. Edward. 1974. "The Exchange Rate and U.S. Agriculture." *American Journal of Agricultural Economics* 56 (February): 1-13.

Timoshenko, V. P. 1938. "Monetary Influences on Postwar Wheat Prices." *Wheat Studies*. Stanford, Calif. Food Research Institute, Stanford University, April.

——. 1975. Agricultural Statistics. Washington, D.C.: Government Printing Office.

U.S. Department of Agriculture. 1976. *Farm Index*. Washington, D.C.: Government Printing Office, October.

——. 1976a. Farm Real Estate Market Developments. Washington, D.C.: Government Printing Office, July.

8

INSULATING TRADE POLICIES, INVENTORIES, AND GRAIN PRICE STABILITY

The wheat model developed here presents a useful framework for analyzing a topic of considerable current interest: grain price stability and buffer stock policies. Interest in these intertwined subjects has been revived largely because of the volatility of grain prices in the 1970s.* The volatility of prices depends on the volume of world trade, therefore the adequacy of a given buffer stock depends on the kind of trade policies pursued by governments. A policy of insulating a country's market from world prices can achieve domestic price stability only by adding to price instability in the rest of the world. In this chapter we analyze the relationship between price variability, inventories, and trade controls in terms of our wheat model. We again use the data from the turbulent year of 1973–74 to examine the implications of the insulating policies pursued in that year.

There has been some confusion, especially in journalistic accounts, between the problems of cyclical fluctuation in production and prices of food and the long-run problem of the availability of food. The specter of large-scale famine, of course, induces not only questions of a humanitarian nature, but those of political stability as well. We are not going to grapple with these global issues. Rather we will attempt to produce some limited evidence on conflicting policy goals and tradeoffs for the short-term cyclical problem. We do need at this point to sketch in more detail than in previous chapters the setting for the reserve problem.

---

*For a discussion of the same issues during the period following World War II, see Johnson (1950, ch. 9).

RECENT EXPERIENCE

From World War II to the early 1970s problems of grain shortages and high prices seldom arose. In the major wheat-exporting nations the dominant concern was the opposite one of how to cope with large stocks and low prices. Domestic price support policies in those countries had led to stockpiling of wheat (see Table 8.1). U.S. and Canadian government stocks varied considerably, but the variation did not follow a systematic buffer stock pattern. In the early 1960s U.S. wheat inventories were approximately equal to one year's production, and by 1969-70 stocks were still 60 percent of annual wheat production. Canada's stocks were even larger, and by 1969-70 they were approximately 150 percent of annual wheat production. One of the effects of these large government inventory operations was to make it unprofitable for private firms and other governments to carry their own inventories. Thus the world experienced a long period without major fluctuations in grain prices.

Although wheat prices did not fluctuate greatly, they tended downward until they reached their trough in 1969 and 1970. At that point the real wheat price in the United States was as low as any year in this century except 1932 (see Table 1.7). By this time the United States and Canada were actively seeking to reduce inventories by production control and export promotion. At one point subsidized exports were 65 percent of total U.S. wheat exports. The International Grains Agreement, which had set a minimum export price for wheat, became defunct as the major exporters sold for less than the agreed minimum price (Johnson 1973, p. 128). Thus in the early 1970s policy makers in the United States and Canada were virorously attempting to reduce excess inventories.

About the time that inventories had been reduced to historically low levels, several new events coincided in 1972-73 to sharply reverse the trend of declining wheat prices. The most widely publicized event was the severe shortfall in Soviet wheat production that resulted in a large increase in imports of 11 million tons. The Soviet purchase from the United States has been called the "great grain robbery" because the sales price was subsidized as part of a zealous export promotion policy that failed to recognize the reversal of world market conditions from surplus to shortage. The real wheat price (in 1967 dollars), which had declined steadily since 1947-48, was $1.32 in 1971-72, and the next year it jumped to $1.80. In 1973-74, despite a record world wheat crop and a decrease in Soviet imports of 11 million tons, real wheat prices doubled to $3.63 ($4.83 in current dollars). Several explanations for the sharp price increase have been offered, including devaluation of the dollar (Schuh 1974), insulating trade policies (Johnson 1975; Johnson, Grennes, and Thursby 1977; Josling 1977) and inadequate inventories.* Because of large-scale inventory decumulation the pre-

---

*The list of explanations is interminable, but for a discussion of some of the others see Sarris, Abbott, and Taylor (1977).

vious year, stocks at the beginning of 1973-74 were the smallest in years, and we attempt to show below the extent to which prevailing trade policies reduced the effectiveness of those stocks.

BUFFER STOCKS

Higher grain prices resulted in political concern about food availability. The extreme concern was famine, but the more pervasive problem was the redistribution of income within and between countries. This political problem resulted in the 1974 World Food Conference in Rome, which endorsed a world grain reserve. In addition, many government and private proposals have been offered (Eaton and Steele 1976; Behrman 1976) including one by the United States (Steele 1976) including one by the United States (Steele 1976). Several of those proposals adovcated a world reserve of 25 million tons of wheat (Trezise 1976). It should be noted that while politicians continue to debate the reserve question, several large harvests have resulted in wheat inventories of 30 million tons in the United States alone by May 1977.*

Both variation in inventories and variation in trade can substitute for price fluctuation (Johnson and Sumner 1976; Reutlinger et al. 1976). A given price increase could be avoided by either a release from inventories or an increase in imports. As a particular inventory policy, a buffer stock can substitute for trade, and we will attempt to measure the degree of substitution. However, we do not intend to discuss the merits of specific buffer stock proposals, since they involve several complex issues that are not our major concern.

One unsettled issue is the optimum degree of price stability.† A second problem involves the relationship between price stability and revenue or income stability, since a policy that stabilizes price does not necessarily stabilize revenue. The precise relationship depends on underlying parameters, and there is some evidence that, in the case of wheat, a policy that would stabilize price would simultaneously destabilize revenue (Behrman 1976). A third issue is the thorny problem of income distribution between consumers and producers within countries and between net importing and net exporting countries. Just as a buffer stock may increase or decrease the variance of revenue, it may also increase or decrease average producer revenue. There is evidence that the revenue effect varies widely across commodities and may involve large magnitudes for products

---

*Some fraction of this figure is working stocks.

†One approach to determining optimum price stability and optimum inventories is presented by Johnson and Sumner (1976) who follow the pioneering work of Gustafson (1958). The objective chosen is to maximize the area under a demand curve minus storage costs, where the perturbations come from random supply fluctuations.

TABLE 8.1

Carryin, Carryout, and Change in Inventories of Wheat, 1964/65–1974/75
(thousand metric tons)

	World[a]			United States			Canada			Australia		
	Carryin	Carryout	Change	Carryin	Carryout	Change	Carryin	Carryout	Change	Carryin	Carryout	Change
1965/66	47,368	35,674	−11,694	22,242	14,565	−7,677	13,962	11,434	−2,528	663	453	−210
1966/67	35,674	37,604	+1,930	14,565	11,551	−3,014	11,434	15,697	+4,263	453	2,191	+1,738
1967/68	37,604	45,481	+7,877	11,551	14,657	+3,106	15,697	18,112	+2,415	2,191	1,402	−789
1968/69	45,522	64,569	+19,047	14,657	22,226	+7,569	18,112	23,183	+5,071	1,402	7,259	+5,857
1969/70	64,569	67,342	+2,773	22,226	24,086	+1,860	23,183	27,452	+4,269	7,259	7,217	−42
1970/71	67,342	52,032	−15,310	24,086	19,894	−4,192	27,452	19,982	−7,470	7,217	3,404	−3,813
1971/72	52,032	51,773	−259	19,894	23,487	+3,593	19,982	15,887	−4,095	3,404	1,448	−1,956
1972/73	51,773	28,966	−22,807	23,487	11,920	−11,567	15,887	9,945	−5,942	1,448	485	−963
1973/74	28,966	27,246	−1,720	11,920	6,722	−5,198	9,945	10,497	+552	485	1,882	−1,397
1974/75	27,074	29,695	+2,612	6,722	8,899	+2,177	10,089	8,037	−2,052	1,887	1,658	−229

	Argentina			EEC-9[b]			Japan		
	Carryin	Carryout	Change	Carryin	Carryout	Change	Carryin	Carryout	Change
1965/66	3,340	175	-3,165	5,587	6,754	+1,167	1,000	975	-25
1966/67	175	245	+70	6,754	5,446	-1,308	975	1,215	+240
1967/68	245	1,008	+763	5,446	7,611	-2,165	1,215	1,050	-165
1968/69	1,008	312	-696	7,652	8,883	+1,231	1,050	1,000	-50
1969/70	312	780	+468	8,883	5,615	-3,268	1,000	860	-140
1970/71	780	675	-105	5,615	6,533	+918	860	950	+90
1971/72	675	486	-189	6,533	8,062	+1,529	950	1,000	+50
1972/73	486	77	-409	8,062	4,612	-3,450	1,000	1,170	+170
1973/74	77	1,013	+936	4,612	5,850	-1,238	1,170	1,110	-60
1974/75	1,013	775	-238	7,363	10,326	+2,963	n.a.	n.a.	n.a.

[a]For United States, Canada, Australia, Argentina, EEC-9, Spain, and Sweden.
[b]Six original member states to 1967/68, thereafter nine member states.
Source: World Wheat Statistics, London: International Wheat Council, 1976. Foreign Agriculture Circular, Grains, U.S. Department of Agriculture, Washington, D.C.: Government Printing Office, May 1976.

such as wheat (Behrman 1976, p. 55). Because of these and related problems, there is no consensus on the proper objectives of inventory policy. However, for any specified objective of inventory policy no matter how it is determined, the optimal level of inventories cannot be determined without reference to a set of trade controls. There are tradeoffs between inventories and trade, and we will attempt to measure this relationship in terms of our model.

QUANTITATIVE EFFECTS OF INVENTORY AND TRADE POLICY

To see the effect of trade policy on inventories, consider an importer such as the EEC or Japan. For a given tariff they may respond to a shortage partly by reducing inventories and partly by increasing imports. However, by reducing the tariff in a time of shortage, they can reduce the need for domestic inventories by relying more on imports. Similarly, exporters such as Canada and Australia could, for a given export tax, satisfy a foreign shortage partly from current production and partly from inventory reduction. By raising the export tax in the face of a shortage they can reduce the need for domestic inventories. Since a given shortage can be met either from imports or inventories, any trade restriction can be translated into an equivalent inventory change.

In terms of the model presented in earlier chapters, a reserve stock purchase can be treated as an exogenous purchase from the country supplying the stock. By looking at a projected exogenous shift in isolation, one can calculate the impact of that shift on each endogenous variable if all other things were held constant. To illustrate the mechanics of the model, consider the effects of a 10 percent increase in U.S. wheat exports to the USSR or any other country in the rest-of-the-world category. This increase in wheat demand would increase the price of domestic wheat in each of the following countries by the stated percentages:

Canada	5.7
Australia	7.0
United States	17.3
Argentina	1.5
Europe	3.5

These numbers indicate that an increase in the demand for U.S. wheat of the above magnitude would have a sizable impact on its own price and on the prices of competitors.

We can utilize our model to analyze the sharp price increase of 1973–74 by incorporating the important exogenous variables. World wheat production increased by nearly 10 percent. Soviet production increased by 20 percent and imports declined by 11 million tons. Because inventory decumulation in Canada and the United States was smaller in 1973-74 than in the previous year, the total market supply of North American wheat declined. Of our endogenous regions only Australia showed an increase in total supply and exports to the rest of the world. In addition world wheat demand was strengthened by the high price of feed grains.

All of these fluctuations in production and inventories were accompanied by policy changes in both exporting and importing countries as they sought to insulate themselves from price changes in the international wheat market. These changes can be entered as exogenous shifters in our model, and their impact on the endogenous flows and prices can be analyzed. The policy changes were discussed at some length in the preceding chapter. Reviewing briefly: Canada and Australia as major exporters put on export taxes, Japan subsidized imports, while the EEC encouraged imports and embargoed exports. These actions left the United States as the only major actor in the wheat market whose domestic price responded to external forces. The results of this activity were shown in Table 7.3. It was shown there that incorporating these policy changes substantially improves the accuracy of the 1973-74 price predictions of the wheat model.

The price increases of 1973-74 could have been avoided if larger inventories had been available. We can use the model to calculate what additional inventory would have been necessary in 1973-74 to keep the U.S. domestic price at its 1972-73 level.* From the underlying structure we can obtain two alternative inventory changes. One is the implied change under constant 1972-73 trade policy and the other is the required change in the presence of the insulating policies of 1973-74. The solutions are found easily by holding all other supplies constant, holding all demand shifts constant, and then including the two sets of price distortions and solving backward for the change in U.S. supply that would have led to no change in the U.S. internal price in the face of the proposed structure.

If we take the constant trade policy case, the required release from inventory that would have kept the internal U.S. price constant was 7.2 percent or 4.197 million metric tons. The effect of the actual 1973-74 policies that shifted world demand onto U.S. wheat was to increase the required release from U.S. inventories to 12.2 percent or 7.099 million tons. This increase of 4 million tons measures the extent to which trade policies rendered actual inventories less productive in terms of stabilizing prices than they otherwise would have been.

An extension of this analysis is to ask what simultaneous inventory changes in all endogenous exporting countries would have produced no change in any

---

*Josling (1977) has measured this effect by calculating equivalent producer and consumer subsidies.

internal price, other things being held constant. In the constant trade policy case the required inventory changes are:

	Percentage	1,000 metric tons
United States	1.0	415
Canada	1.3	350
Australia	-9.7	-1,217
Argentina	10.6	704
Europe	7.0	3,558
		3,810

In the case of actual 1973-74 policies inventory changes are:

	Percentage	1,000 metric tons
United States	8.7	5,070
Canada	-3.1	-829
Australia	-26.0	-3,266
Argentina	10.7	713
Europe	8.8	4,461
		6,149

These calculations imply that a net addition to supply from inventories of 3.8 million metric tons in the absence of policy changes would have stabilized prices at the previous year's level for the major exporting countries. This quantity represents approximately 2.5 percent of the total supply of the exporters in 1973-74. In the case of the policies that actually prevailed in that year, a net addition of 6.1 million metric tons to supply would have been required to stabilize prices at the previous year's level. This quantity represents about 4.0 percent of the exporters supply in 1973-74. The difference of more than 2 million tons measures the extent to which trade policies reduced the productivity of world inventories in terms of price stabilization.

Several inferences can be drawn from the preceding analysis. With regard to stabilizing the price in the United States and prices in other exporting countries, the required release from inventories is larger with the actual trade policies of 1973-74 than with the hypothetical 1972-73 policies. With regard to stabilizing the U.S. price alone, a second inference is that if all countries simultaneously pursue inventory policies that stabilize prices, the required release from U.S. inventories is smaller than if the U.S. is acting alone. With constant 1972-73 trade policies, concerted action reduces the required U.S. release from 7.2 percent to 1 percent. With actual 1973-74 policies the required U.S. release is reduced from 12.2 percent to 8.7 percent. Thus we have shown the size of the inventory needed to stabilize prices both when the United States acts alone and when the major exporters act in concert. In addition the stabilization job requires more inventories when insulating trade policies are pursued, and we have attempted to measure this trade-off.

CONCLUSION

The world wheat market had a turbulent year in 1973-74. Consumers and their governments may have been unusually sensitive to higher prices because of price increases in the previous year associated with large-scale Soviet imports. Whatever the cause, many governments around the world acted to insulate consumers from higher prices abroad. Importing nations reduced tariffs and subsidized imports. Exporting nations employed export taxes, quotas, and embargoes to keep their wheat at home. Of course all countries cannot engage in insulation if the world market is to clear, so the net effect of insulation by some countries is to shift adjustment onto the remaining countries. Much of the adjustment fell on the U.S. market, which remained relatively open. Our calculations show that the percentage increase in the U.S. price was at least twice as large as it would have been had its partners pursued the trade policies of the previous year. Alternatively the United States could have avoided the wheat price increase in the face of insulation by its partners if the United States had held larger inventories.

We make no recommendation here on the wisdom of various grain reserve proposals. Our message is that trade and inventories are substitutes and that the relationship is too close to ignore with impunity. Attempts to separate the issues may result in costly errors.

REFERENCES

Behrman, Jere. 1976. "International Commodity Agreements." Paper prepared for the Overseas Development Council, mimeographed.

Eaton, David J. and W. Scott Steele, eds. 1976. *Analyses of Grain Reserves: A Proceedings.* Washington, D.C.: U.S. Department of Agriculture, Economic Research Service Report No. 634.

Gustafson, Robert L. Carryover Levels for Grains: A Method for Determining Amounts that are Optional under Specified Conditions, USDA technical bulletin no. 1178, Washington, D.C.: Government Printing Office, October 1958.

Johnson, D. Gale. 1950. *Trade and Agriculture: A Study of Inconsistent Policies.* New York: Wiley.

———. 1973. *World Agriculture in Disarray.* London: Macmillan.

———. 1975. "World Agriculture, Commodity Policy, and Price Variability." *American Journal of Agricultural Economics* 57 (December): 823-28.

Johnson, D. Gale and Daniel Sumner. 1976. "An Optimization Approach to Grain Reserves for Developing Countries." In Eaton and Steele.

Johnson, Paul R., Thomas Grennes, and Marie Thursby. 1977. "Devaluation, Foreign Trade Controls, and Domestic Wheat Prices." *American Journal of Agricultural Economics* 59 (November).

Josling, T. 1977. "Agricultural Portection and Stabilization Policies: An Analysis of Current Neo-Mercantilist Practices." Paper presented to the Symposium on International Trade and Agriculture, Tucson, Ariz.

International Wheat Council. 1976. *World Wheat Statistics*. London.

Reutlinger, Shlomo, David Eaton, David Bigman, and David Blum. 1976. "Should Developing Countries Carry Grain Reserves?" In Eaton and Steele.

Sarris, Alexander H., Phillip C. Abbott, and Lance Taylor. 1977. "Grain Reserves, Emergency Relief, and Food Aid." Report prepared for the Overseas Development Council, mimeographed.

Schuh, G. Edward. 1974. "The Exchange Rate and U.S. Agriculture." *American Journal of Agricultural Economics* 56 (February): 1-13.

Steele, W. Scott. 1976. "Alternative Approaches to Stabilizing International Markets." *Southern Journal of Agricultural Economics* 8 (July): 57-62.

Trezise, Phillip H. 1976. *Rebuilding Grain Reserves: Toward an International System*. Washington, D.C.: Brookings Institution.

U.S. Department of Agriculture. 1976. *Foreign Agriculture Circular, Grains*. Washington, D.C.: Government Printing Office, May.

INDEX

F

feed grains (see, coarse grains)
Floyd, John, 113-14, 115
Forrester, Jay W., 27-29
freight rates (see, transport
    costs

G

Giffen paradox, 11
grain prices, 1, 16-19, 117-25

H

Heckscher, Eli F., 12-13

I

impact multipliers, 77-78
import shares, 55
insulating trade policies, 16-19,
    106, 109, 110-13, 118, 123
inventories, 17-18, 117-25

J

Japan, 5, 38, 44, 84, 98, 109
Johnson, D. Gale, 15, 117,
    118-19
Johnson, Paul R., 22
Josling, Timothy, 123

L

land prices, 113-16
livestock, 85

M

marketing margins, 42, 43
Marshall, Alfred, 11-12
Meadows, Donella, 27-29

N

naive models: coarse grains,
    93; wheat, 66
Nordhaus, William D., 27-29

P

protective policy, 14, 15-17
provision policy, 12-14

Q

quality of data, 77, 101-04

R

reduced-form model, 21,
    28-30
Resnick, Stephen A., 24, 34
Rhomberg, Rudolf, 33
rice, 2, 84, 93-106
Rojko, Anthony, 23-24, 27,
    54, 55, 101
Rome, ancient: trade policy
    of, 11, 13

S

Schmitz, Andrew, 22-25
Schuh, G. Edward, 106, 114

shipping costs (see, transport
    costs
Smith, Adam, 11, 13, 19
South Africa, 84
South Asia, 98
Southeast Asia, 98
spatial equilibrium models, 21-28,
    33, 55-59
systems dynamics model, 21, 27

T

Thailand, 84
trade controls, 41, 42-47 (see
    also, export subsidies,
    insulating trade policies,
    protective policy, provision
    policy)
transport costs, 14, 41, 42-47,
    78, 109-10, 113-14
Truman, Edwin, 24, 34

U

United States, 2, 5, 8, 38, 84,
    93; grain agreement with

USSR, 15, 19, 110
USSR, 2, 7, 18-19, 74, 118;
    grain agreement with United
    States, 110
utility maximization: two-stage
p   process of, 47-48

V

variable levy (see, European
    Economic Community)

W

wheat: cross elasticity of
    demand (coarse grains)
    for, 60; demand for,
    38; feed use, 3; income
    elasticity of demand for,
    3; international agree-
    ment, 16; price elasticity
    of demand for, 39, 40,
    80; prices, 10, 107,
    110-13; supply of, 40;
    types of, 1-3

ABOUT THE AUTHORS

THOMAS GRENNES is currently on the faculty of the Department of Economics, North Carolina State University. He has studied at Indiana University, the University of Wisconsin, and the University of Chicago. His publications have appeared in the Southern Economic Journal and the American Journal of Agricultural Economics. He has written on the subjects of international finance, trade in agricultural products, and energy.

PAUL R. JOHNSON is Professor of Economics and Business at North Carolina State University. He earned his A.B. degree at Oberlin College and his Ph. D. degree at the University of Chicago. He has published articles on related subjects in the American Journal of Agricultural Economics, the Economic Record, the Journal of Econometrics, and the Southern Economic Journal.

MARIE CURRIE THURSBY is Assistant Professor of Economics at Syracuse University. Her B.A. degree was earned at Mount Holyoke College and her Ph. D. degree at the University of North Carolina. Her articles have appeared in the Economic Journal and the American Journal of Agricultural Economics.

AGRICULTURAL SUPPLY RESPONSE: A Survey of
the Econometric Evidence

Hossein Askari
John Thomas Cummings

*FOREIGN TRADE AND U.S. POLICY: The Case for
Free International Trade

Leland B. Yeager
David G. Tuerck

THE POLITICAL ECONOMY OF EAST-WEST TRADE
Connie M. Friesen

SOVIET AGRICULTURE: An Assessment of Its
Contributions to Economic Development

edited by
Harry G. Shaffer

WORLD FOOD PROSPECTS AND AGRICULTURAL
POTENTIAL

Marylin Chou
David P. Harmon, Jr.
Herman Kahn

*Also available in paperback as a PSS Student Edition.